A
GUIDE
TO
CONVEYANCING RESIDENTIAL
PROPERTY
THE EASYWAY

ALAN STEWART

Easyway Guides

D0260478

ISBN
978-1-84716-605-0

Printed in Great Britain by 4 edge www.4edge.co.uk

Cover design by Straightforward Graphics

This book was accurate at the time of going to press. The information within reflects the nature of the publication. The author and publisher cannot be held liable for any errors and omissions in the book that may cause others to incur loss.

The book has been written on the strict understanding that it is a guide to the process of conveyancing and should not be used to replace a professional conveyancer.

Contents

Introduction

Index

Appendix

1. Sample conveyancing costs when using a licensed conveyancer

2. Standard letters used in conveyancing

3. Standard forms used in basic conveyancing

****

INTRODUCTION

This book is not a substitute for a qualified professional and is not presented as such. The information contained within is for use as guidance and at all times the advice of professionals should be sought, as only the extremely confident and experienced lay person, or actual practitioner can buy or sell property alone.

Usually, when buying or selling residential property, solicitors or licensed conveyancers are normally used in order to ensure that the transaction proceeds smoothly. Both are regulated professionals whose governing bodies require that they be insured and properly regulated. Licensed conveyancers are regulated by the Council of Licensed Conveyancers, solicitors by the Solicitors Regulation Authority or Law Society. Both carry out the process of buying and selling property in a similar way. There are several legal differences between the professions. Conveyancers are allowed to represent both buyer and seller, whereas solicitors generally don't because of conflict of interest. Similarly, licensed conveyancers need not tell their client if they have received a commission from a marketing or referral agency, whereas solicitors must disclose such commissions. In general, licensed conveyancers may be more suited to a lower value or uncomplicated sale-and it will be much cheaper. If the sale is complex and expensive then a solicitor will be better suited.

However, the actual processes of conveyancing are usually a mystery to both buyer and seller who are not privy to the procedures. The aim of this brief but concise book is to throw some light on the basic processes, thus ensuring that those who are involved at least have some understanding of what is happening and can question those acting for them at any given point. The book should be read in conjunction with "A Straightforward Guide to Buying and Selling Property" which deals with the more general aspects such as the involvement of estate agents.

Although it is safe to say that the average basic conveyance of a leasehold flat or freehold house is relatively simple and unproblematic, there are still fundamental ground rules which one must observe.

When purchasing a leasehold flat for example, particularly in a multi-occupied block, the lease has to be very closely scrutinised and all the covenants in the lease understood. Leases can be unintelligible documents, couched in redundant language, badly laid out and misleading at the best of times.

Leases contain landlord and tenants covenants, which impose rights and obligations on the respective parties, particularly in relation to repairing obligations and service charge and ground rent payments. Other covenants may impose an onerous burden on the leaseholder and quite often only an experienced eye can pick this up.

Likewise, the freehold transfer document may contain obligations, which can only be picked up or understood, by an experienced eye.

Therefore, even if you decide to carry out conveyancing yourself you should always get a sound second opinion concerning the lease or freehold document.

What about online conveyancing?

Traditionally homebuyers have used local solicitors or conveyancers, often recommended by their estate agent or mortgage lender (see below). However, online conveyancing is a growing area that is transforming the industry – generally for the better. Online conveyancing companies sell their services over the web, usually backed up by a call centre. They are often based in business parks and are effectively warehouses of fully trained conveyancers dealing with thousands of property transactions. They are usually much more efficient and better value as a result of economies of scale and not being based in city centres. Like ordinary solicitors, the quality of service can be mixed. You deal with them via email and telephone and never see them face to face. Some online conveyancers' business model means your file is on a system and you talk to different people each time. This can be frustrating. Others allocate your file to one person which provides you with a point of contact. Good online conveyancers should enable you to access your file 24/7, so you can see its progress. This is useful because when sellers badger buyers for updates you can tell them immediately. Be aware that many websites describe themselves as online conveyancing, but are actually just price comparison websites which will get quotes for you from third party conveyancers or solicitors. This can be very helpful in finding a cheap service, but you can't be sure about sort of quality of service you are going to get from whoever you end up with. However, conveyancers – whether online or not – cannot deal with complex legal issues, and you should then go with a solicitor -

As we will see later, there are two forms of conveyancing in existence, registered and unregistered. The former means that the ownership of land and all that entails, including extent of ownership, is registered at the Land Registry. The very fact of registration ensures that legal title can be verified. Unregistered land has to be proven through production of deeds, which can be time consuming and problematic. Land Registration has been compulsory in the United Kingdom for a while now, but it is still a fact that a fairly significant amount of all property is unregistered.

This book details the processes of conveyancing as it affects both registered and unregistered land. It then goes on to deal with the advanced stages of conveyancing as it affects unregistered land and also the process of conveying registered land.

Following the conclusion, there is a glossary of terms and a list of useful addresses. There is an appendix, which outlines Land Registry forms currently in use for conveyancing property.

Finally this book cannot guarantee that you will be in a position to convey property without expert help, precisely because it is a guide to conveyancing. However, it should enlighten you as to the processes.

****

1

CONVEYANCING IN CONTEXT

Conveyancing, or the practice of conveyancing, is about how to transfer the ownership of land and property from one person or organisation to another. Land and property can include freehold property, leasehold property (residential) or can include business leases. It is principally the conveyance of residential property that this book is concerned with.

Essentially, the process of conveyancing lays down clear procedures for the conveyancer and also sets out each party's position during the sale or acquisition.

Before understanding the process of conveyancing, however, it is essential to understand something about the legal forms of ownership of property.

Legal ownership of property

There are two main forms of legal ownership of property in England and Wales If you are about to embark on the sale or acquisition of a house or flat (or business) then you will be dealing in the main with either freehold or leasehold property.

It is very rare indeed to find other forms of ownership, although, with the advent of the Commonhold and Leasehold Reform Act 2002, which became law in May 2002, the government introduced a form of ownership called 'common hold' that in essence, creates the freehold ownership of flats, with common responsibility for communal areas.

Freehold property

In general, if you own the freehold of a house or a piece of land, then you will be the outright owner with no fixed period of time and no one else to answer to (with the exception of statutory authorities).

There may be registered restrictions on title, which we will be discussing later. The property will probably be subject to a mortgage so the only other overriding interest will be that of the bank or the building society. The responsibility for repairs, maintenance and general upkeep will be the freeholders. The law can intervene if certain standards are not maintained.

The deed to your house will be known as the "freehold transfer document" which will contain any rights and obligations. Usually, the transfer document will list any "encumbrances" (restrictions) on the use of the land, such as rights of way of other parties, sales restrictions etc. The deeds to your home are the most important documentation. As we will see later, without deeds and historical data, such as the proof of title, it can be rather complicated selling property. This is why the system of land registration in use in this country has greatly simplified property transactions.

Any person owning freehold property is free to create another interest in land, such as a lease or a weekly or monthly tenancy, subject to any restrictions the transfer may contain.

Leasehold property

If a person lives in a property owned by someone else and has an agreement for a period of time, usually a long period, over 21 years and up to 99 years or 125 years, and in some cases 999 years, then they are a leaseholder. The conveyancing of leasehold property is potentially, far more problematic than freehold property, particularly when the flat is in a block with a number of units.

The lease is a contract between landlord and tenant which lays down the rights and obligations of both parties and should be read thoroughly by both the leaseholder and, in particular, the conveyancer. Once signed then the purchaser is bound by all the clauses in the contract.

It is worth looking at the nature of a lease before discussing the rather more complex process of conveyancing. Again, it has to be stated that it is of the utmost importance that both the purchaser and the vendor understand the nature of a lease.

The lease

Preamble

The start of a lease is called the preamble. This defines the landlord and purchaser and also the nature of the property in question (the demise). It will also detail the remaining period of the lease.

Leaseholders covenants

Covenants are best understood as obligations and responsibilities. Leaseholder's covenants are therefore a list of things that leaseholders should do, such as pay their service charges and keep the interior of the dwelling in good repair and not, for example, to alter the structure. The landlord's covenants will set out the obligations of the landlord, which is usually to maintain the structure and exterior of the block and light common parts etc. One unifying theme of all leasehold property is that, notwithstanding the landlord's responsibilities, it is the leaseholder who will pay for everything out of a service charge.

Leases will make detailed provisions for the setting, managing and charging of service charges which should include a section on accounting. All landlords of leaseholders are accountable under the Landlord and Tenant Act 1985, as amended by the 1987 Act and the 2002 Commonhold and Leasehold reform Act. These Acts will regulate the way a landlord treats a leaseholder in the charging and accounting of service charges.

In addition, the 1996 Housing Act and the Commonhold and Leasehold Reform Act 2002 have provided further legislation protecting leaseholders by introducing the right of leaseholders to go to Leasehold Valuation Tribunals if they are unhappy with levels and management of charges and also to carry out audits of charges.

It is vital when buying a leasehold property that you read the lease. Leases tend to be different from each other and nothing can be assumed. When you buy a property, ensure that the person selling has paid all debts and has contributed to some form of "sinking fund" whereby provision has been built up for major repairs in the future. Make sure that you will not be landed with big bills after moving in and that if you are, there is money to deal with them. After a lease has been signed then there is little or no recourse to recoup any money owed.

These are all the finer points of leases and the conveyancer has to be very vigilant. In particular read the schedules to the lease as these sometimes contain rather more detail.

One of the main differences between leasehold and freehold

property is that the lease is a long tenancy agreement which contains provisions that give the landlord rather a lot of power to manage (or mismanage) and it is always a possibility that a leaseholder can be forced to give up his or her home in the event of non-compliance with the terms of the lease. This is known as forfeiture.

Under the Commonhold and Leasehold Reform Act 2002 referred to earlier, a new 'no fault right to manage' has been introduced. This will enable leaseholders who are unhappy with the management of their property, to take over the management with relative ease. The Act will apply to most landlords, with the exception of local authorities.

These new powers will go a long way to curb the excesses or inefficiencies of numerous landlords and will provide more control and greater security for leaseholders.

Check points

There are key areas of a lease that should be checked when purchasing. Some have already been discussed.

- What is the term left on the lease?
- Is the preamble clear, i.e. is the area which details landlord, tenant and demised (sold) premises clear?
- Is the lease assignable, i.e. can you pass on the lease without landlords permission or does it need surrendering at sale or a license to assign?
- What is the ground rent and how frequently will you pay it?
- What is the level of service charge, if any, and how is it collected, apportioned, managed and accounted for?

- What are the general restrictions in the lease, can you have pets for example, can you park cars, do you have a designated space?
- What are the respective repairing obligations? As we have seen, the leaseholder will pay anyway but the landlord and leaseholder will hold respective responsibilities. This is an important point because occasionally, there is no stated responsibility for upkeep and the environment deteriorates as a consequence, diminishing the value of the property.

Business leases

Generally, the Landlord and Tenant Act 1954, part 2, provides the framework for those occupying premises on the basis of a business lease. There are a few exceptions to this such as mining leases and agricultural leases. The average business lease will be shorter than a residential lease and will contain periodic rent review clauses. The typical business lease may be for ten years with a rent review after the fifth year.

The whole process of conveyancing business leases, although similar to residential in some respects, is rather more complex. For example, maintenance rights and responsibilities are often an issue between the parties concerned and it is essential that there is a clear picture at the outset. Those coming to the end of the term of their leases can find themselves faced with a significant repair bill, based on a schedule of dilapidations undertaken by a surveyor.

As with all leases, it is very important to ensure that those managing have a firm and comprehensive grasp over the whole process. If they do not then this can affect the value of the property when you wish to sell or buy a lease. It is not advised that an individual undertakes this type of conveyancing, but employs a solicitor well versed in the finer points of business tenancies. 'A Straightforward Guide to Managing Commercial Property', deals with business tenancies in more depth.

Two systems of conveyancing

After gaining an understanding of the nature of the interest in land that you are buying, it is absolutely essential to understand the two systems of conveyancing property in existence, as this will determine, not so much the procedure because the initial basic steps in conveyancing, such as carrying out searches, are common to both forms of land, registered and unregistered, but the way you go about the process and the final registration.

Registered and unregistered land

In England and Wales the method of conveyancing to be used in each particular transaction very much depends on whether the land is registered or unregistered land. If the title, or proof of ownership, of land and property has been registered under the Land Registration Acts 1925-86, as amended, then the Land Registry (see below) will be able to furnish the would-be conveyancer with such documentation as is required to establish ownership, or third party rights etc. If the land has not been registered then proof of ownership of the land in question must be traced through the title deeds.

Registered land

All conveyancing falls within the remit of the Land Registry, because it is compulsory to register land throughout England and Wales. The Land Registration Acts of 1925 established the Land Registry (HM

Land Registry). The Land Registry is a department of the Civil Service, at its head is the Chief Land Registrar. Anybody can obtain information which is held on the register of a registered title by going to www.landregistry-search.com. There is a list of fees on this site for the various searches.

There is specific terminology in use within conveyancing, particularly within the Land Registry:

a) A piece of land, or parcel of land is known as a registered title.
b) The owner of land is referred to as the registered proprietor.
c) A conveyance of registered land is called a transfer.
d) A transaction involving registered land is known as a dealing.

The main difference between the two types of conveyancing registered and unregistered concerns what is known as proof of title. In the case of land that is unregistered the owner will prove title by showing the would-be purchaser the documentary evidence which shows how he or she came to own the land and property.

In the case of registered land the owner has to show simply that he or she is registered at the Land Registry as the registered proprietor. Proof of registration is proof of ownership, which is unequivocal. In registered land the documents proving ownership are replaced by the fact of registration. Each separate title or ownership of land has a title number, which the Land Registry uses to trace or confirm ownership. The description of each title on the register is identified by the title number, described by reference to the filed plan (indicating limits and extent of ownership). With registered conveyancing the Land Registry keeps the register of title and file plan. The owner (proprietor) is issued with a Land Certificate. If the land in question is subject to a mortgage then the mortgagor is issued with a Land Certificate.

Production of the Land Certificate

Before the introduction of the Land Registration Act 2002, with registered land, whenever there is a sale, or disposition, then the Land Certificate had to be produced to the Land Registry in the appropriate district. The Land Registry no longer produces land or charge certificates.

Now read the key points from chapter 1 overleaf.

****

KEY POINTS FROM CHAPTER ONE

- Conveyancing is about how to transfer the ownership of land and property from one person to another.

- The process of conveyancing lays down clear procedures for the conveyancer and also sets out each party's position during the process.

- There are two systems of conveyancing-that dealing with registered land and that dealing with unregistered land. Proof of title is easier to establish when land is registered.

- It is compulsory throughout England and Wales to register land- in spite of this a significant amountt of land remains unregistered.

KEY STEPS IN CONVEYANCING – THE INITIAL BASIC SEARCHES

2

THE KEY STEPS IN THE PROCESS OF CONVEYANCING PROPERTY – BASIC SEARCHES

Searches

In chapter's three and four, we will be looking specifically at the processes of conveyancing as they affect registered and unregistered land. However, before we do, it is necessary to look at the processes generally, in order to form a clear idea.

Before the buyer exchanges contracts on a property and then completes the purchase, a number of searches are always carried out. In this chapter we will be looking at four key searches:

1   Enquiries before contract.
2   Local land charges search.
3   Enquiries of the local authority.
4   Index map search.

These are the most essential and common searches and a number of the searches are carried out by the seller. Most searches today can be carried out online, for which there is a fee. You should first go to the relevant local authority web page.

Enquiries before contract

These are inquiries to the seller, or the vendor of the property and are aimed at revealing certain facts about the property that the seller has no legal obligation to disclose to the buyer. There are certain matters which are always raised. These are:

- Whether there are any existing boundary disputes.
- What services are supplied to the property, whether electricity, gas or other.
- Any easements or covenants in the lease. These are stipulations in the lease which give other certain rights, such as rights of way.
- Any guarantees in existence.
- Planning considerations.
- Adverse rights affecting the property.
- Any fixtures and fittings.
- Whether there has been any breach of restriction affecting the property.

Please refer to appendix 1 for a sample Purchase statement which lists all the likely charges associated with a purchase of a property when using a solicitor or licensed conveyancer.

The seller's property information forms

If the property is newly built, information will be required concerning any outstanding works or future guarantees of remedying defects. Where a property is leasehold, information will be required about the lessor.

Registered conveyancers will use a standard form to raise these enquiries, so that the initial search is exhaustive. As part of the move towards openness in the process of buying and selling property, and also an attempt to speed up the process of sale, the Law Society introduced forms which the solicitor, or buyer if carrying out his or her own conveyancing, is being encouraged to use. These are Seller's Property Information Form TA6 and TA7 for leasehold information if leasehold. Requisition on title forms are also used. The Law Society Website will give information on what forms are currently used in addition to the aforementioned.

These forms can be obtained from a legal stationers, such as Oyez or, in most cases, from the Land Registry website. See appendix 1 for examples of these forms.

Answers given by the vendor do not form part of the subsequent contract and therefore cannot be used against that person in the event of future problems. However, the Misrepresentations Act of 1976 could be evoked if a deliberate misrepresentation has caused problems.

Local land charges search
The Local Land Charges Act 1975 requires District Councils, London Borough Councils and the City of London Corporation to maintain a Local Land Charges Registry for the area.

Local land charges can be divided into two areas:
1) Financial charges on the land for work carried out by the local authority
2) Restrictions on the use of land

The register is further divided into twelve parts:

a) General financial charges.
b) Specific financial charges.
c) Planning charges.
d) Miscellaneous charges and provisions.
e) Charges for improvements of ways over fenland.
f) Land compensation charges.
g) New town charges.
h) Civil aviation charges.
i) Open cast coal mining charges.
j) Listed buildings charges.
k) Light obstruction notices.
l) Drainage scheme charges.

All charges are enforceable by the local authority except g and i, which are enforced by statutory bodies and private individuals generally.

A buyer should search in all parts of this particular register and this can be done by a personal or official search. A personal search, as the name suggests, involves the individual or their agent attending at the local authority office, and on paying the relevant fee, personally searching the register. The charges are registered against the land concerned and not against the owner. The official search is the one most favored because, in the event of missing a vital piece of information the chances of compensation are far higher than with a personal search.

With the official search a requisition for a search and for an official certificate of search is sent to the Registrar of Local Land Charges for the area within which the land is situated. There is a fee and the search is carried out by the Registrars staff, which results in a certificate being sent to the person making the request, which clearly outlines any charges.

The Registrar may require a plan of the land as well as the postal address. Separate searches are made of each parcel of land being purchased.

Local authority enquiries

There is a standard form in use for these particular types of searches. This is known as "Con 29R England and Wales" revised August 2007, and the CON290 Optional enquiries of local authorities, with the format of the form differing slightly for inner London boroughs. Any of the forms in the process can be obtained from legal stationers such as Oyez. They can also be purchased from the Law Society.

The standard forms in use contain a statement to the effect that the local authority is not responsible for errors unless negligence is proved. Many of the inquiries relate specifically to planning matters, whilst other elements of the search are concerned about roads and whether they are adopted and whether there are likely to be any costs falling onto property owners. We will be considering planning matters concerning the individual property a little later. Other inquiries relate to possible construction of new roads which may effect the property, the location of sewers and pipes and whether the property is in an area of compulsory registration of title, a smoke controlled area or slum clearance area.

The form used is so constructed that part 2 of the form contains questions, which must be initialed by the purchaser before they are answered. Again these questions cover planning and other matters. Other enquiries can be made by the individual, which are answered at the authorities discretion. In addition to the above, which are the major searches, there are others that the conveyancer has to be aware of. These are as follows:

Searches in the Index map and parcels index of the Land Register

If the land has been registered the title will be disclosed and whether it is registered, leasehold or freehold. Registered rent charges are also disclosed by the search. (See chapter 7)

Commons Registration Act (1965) search

This act imposes a duty on county councils to keep a register relating to village greens and common land and interests over them, such as right of way.

Coal mining search

The request for this search if relevant, is designed to reveal the whereabouts of mineshafts and should be sent to the local area coal board office, or its equivalent. The search will disclose past workings and any subsidence, proposed future workings and the proximity of opencast workings. It is usually well known if there is a problem, or potential problem with coal mining in an area and this search is essential if that is the case.

Other enquiries

There are a number of other bodies from which it might be appropriate to request a search. These include British Rail, Statutory undertakers such as electricity, water and gas boards, planning authorities generally, rent assessment committees and so on. These will only usually be necessary if there is a direct link between the property being purchased and a particular circumstance within an area or property.

Chancel searches

Chancel repair search – to ensure there are no potential leftover medieval liabilities on the property to help pay for church repairs. This is a necessity and costs £18. However, you may decide to take out Chancel repair insurance instead for £20 or so. The laws around Chancel repair changed in October 2013 so now the onus is on the Church to establish and lodge liability with the Land Registry.

Planning matters relating to specific properties

It is obviously very necessary to determine whether or not any illegal alterations have been carried out to the property you wish to purchase, before reaching the point of exchange of contracts. This is to ensure that the vendor has complied with relevant planning legislation, if any material changes have been made, and that you will not be required at a later date to carry out remedial work. The local authority maintains a register of planning applications relating to properties within their boundaries. In addition, the register will also reveal any planning enforcement notices in force against a particular property.

Questions such as these, and also any questions relating to the effect of structure or local plans, (specific plans relating to local and borough wide plans for the future) should be made in writing to the local authority or an individual search can be carried out. Usually they are carried out if there is any suspicion that planning regulations may have been breached. In addition, there may be other considerations, such as whether the building is listed or whether tree preservation orders relating to trees within the cartilage of the property are in force. It is certainly essential to know about these.

It is highly recommended that all of these searches are carried out and completed before contracts are exchanged.

Environmental searches

Environmental Search – this report is used on the vast majority of transactions and is provided by either Landmark or Groundsure. Depending which product your solicitor usually uses, the report will give information about contaminated land at or around the property, landfill sites, former and current industry, detailed flooding predictions, radon gas hazard, ground stability issues, and some other related information. The cost should be around £50 to £60 including VAT.

Optional and specific locational searches

Optional and location specific searches – sometimes extra searches are required or recommended depending on the location or type of property or due to particular concerns raised by the buyer. These could include:

- Tin Mining searches in Cornwall

- Mining searches in various parts of the UK and Cheshire Brine searches

- Additional Local Authority Questions such as Public Paths, Pipelines, Noise Abatement Zones, Common Land, etc.

Now read the key points from chapter two.

****

KEY POINTS FROM CHAPTER TWO

- Before the buyer exchanges contracts on a property it is essential to carry out a number of key searches.

- In addition to the main searches, there are a number of ancillary searches which should be made if appropriate.

- There are standard forms for carrying out such searches-if you are doing your own conveyancing these can be obtained from any legal stationers, such as Oyez.

- There may be other considerations such as conservation or planning issues that need to be looked into.

3

THE STRUCTURAL SURVEY-The National House Builders Council (Buildmark)

Anyone who purchases a property should carry out a structural survey. This is highly advisable and preferably will be as in-depth as possible. A chartered surveyor should be used. If a qualified surveyor is negligent when compiling his or her report of the property then that person can be sued. Most residential property is purchased with assistance from a building society or bank. The lender will insist on a survey before lending the money in order to protect their advance. However, this survey is cursory at the best and will not reveal more serious problems. Therefore, at this point in the conveyancing process, the person purchasing, or the person acting on his or her behalf should ensure that they are thoroughly acquainted with the condition of the property. If you are purchasing a house which is in the course of construction, then there will be the benefit of a warranty of good work and proper materials so that the house will be fit for habitation. This protection does not extend to any subsequent purchasers. There is however, a form of statutory protection under the Defective Premises Act of 1972 which imposes a duty on a developer and those associated with the developer to build in a correct manner. The Act covers anyone acquiring an interest in a dwelling.

The National House Builders Scheme

This scheme was redrafted in 1979 and in 1988 the Buildmark scheme was introduced. Builders who are registered with the NHBS must offer a warranty to first and subsequent purchasers, that, essentially, has a ten-year shelf life from date of construction. During the first two years from issue the builder is liable to make good any defects due to non-compliance with NHBS regulations. The first two years are known as the initial guarantee period. After this, the remaining eight years are referred to as the structural guarantee period. During this time the NHBS will reimburse the purchaser the cost of remedying major works caused by any defect in the structure or subsidence, settlement or heave, provided that there is no other insurance at the time of the claim to cover the cost.

Liability of the builder outside the two year period

The NHBS agreement states that if any work undertaken by the builder in the initial guarantee period to remedy a defect caused by the breach of the NHBS requirements fails to remedy the defect or damage, the vendor/builder will remain under a continuing liability to remedy the damage after the initial guarantee period.

Conveyancing a property is not just about successfully reaching a conclusion in a sale. It is also about ensuring that the property you are buying is sound and that you make sure that you have a clear picture of what you are buying, preferably by obtaining a report from a chartered surveyor.

Now read the key points from chapter three.

KEY POINTS FROM CHAPTER THREE

- Anyone who purchases a property must carry out a structural survey. It is essential that a qualified surveyor is used.

- If you are purchasing a house under construction there will be the benefit of a warranty with the property.

- The National House Builders Scheme offers a warranty for ten years for those who purchase a house/flat from a registered developer.

PROOF OF TITLE AND OTHER SEARCHES – UNREGISTERED LAND

4

CONVEYANCING UNREGISTERED LAND

We have considered the processes of conveyancing generally and the searches common to all property. However, it is now necessary to look at the specifics of conveyancing registered and unregistered land.

With unregistered land, as we have seen, there is a duty on the vendor to prove his or her title to the land, i.e., that they own the land in question. If all is registered at the Land Registry then life can be a good deal simpler. However, if not, then the process can be more complex.

The abstract of title - unregistered land. Establishing proof of ownership

The abstract of title is an epitome of the various documents and events which together demonstrate that the vendor has good title to the land, conclusively owns the land. The vendor must, at his or her own expense, produce and deliver a proper abstract of title to the purchaser, unless there is an agreement to do otherwise, which would be unusual.

The abstract starts with the root or the origin of title. Every deed which dealt with transactions relating to this property subsequently must be abstracted. A conveyance relating to the purchase of the freehold is the strongest form of root of title, likewise a mortgage deed relating to that conveyance. If a vendor has lost any of the titles which relate to the land then it is usual for the vendor to insert a special condition into the contract stating what secondary evidence will be produced to prove title. Secondary evidence can be in the form of a counterpart lease, for example.

Once the abstract has been delivered, the purchaser must examine these documents against the originals. The purpose of the examination is to ensure that what has been abstracted has been properly or correctly abstracted, ensure that each document has been properly executed, attested and stamped and that there have been no changes to the title, such as memoranda endorsed on deeds or documents. Any doubt as to the validity of the title should be raised with the vendor's solicitor directly and promptly by written requisition. The purchaser is entitled to raise requisitions on any part of the title which is unsatisfactory, for example, if the title discloses a mortgage or covenant which was not disclosed in the contract. An omission from the abstract may be remedied by an answer to the requisition. The expense of verification of this answer is the purchaser's. The purchaser can serve a notice on the vendor requiring him to furnish an answer by a given date. Failure to reply by this date entitles the purchaser to rescind the contract. If the purchaser is still not satisfied with the vendor's replies, he or she can send observations back to the vendor relating to the reply.

There is a standard condition of sale, which states that the vendor can rescind the sale if he or she cannot furnish a reasonable reply to the requisition. This right however, is based on reasonable grounds, i.e., inability or unwillingness to answer.

Pre-completion searches

We discussed the key searches to be carried out prior to exchange and completion in the previous chapter. There are, however, other searches necessary, depending on the status of the property. With unregistered property, some of these searches involve the Land Registry.

The purchaser or agent should carry out various searches immediately before completion in order to determine whether there are any encumbrances affecting the vendor's title to the property. The most important of these is the Land Charges Register of the Land Charges Department of the Land Registry.

There are five registers in total:

a) The register of pending actions. This registers any actions that may be pending against that title.

b) The register of annuities. This registers any rent charge or other charge such as an annuity against the land.

c) The registry of writs and orders. This register is concerned with the registering and enforcing of any orders against land.

d) The register of deeds and arrangements. This is concerned with trustees or creditors who may benefit from that particular title.

e) The register of land charges.

The Register of Land charges

This is the most important register and the charges are classified as follows:

a) Class A (s2(2). These are charges upon land, created by statute, which only come into existence after the appropriate person has made an application under the particular statute. Once created they may be registered against the estate owner.

b) Class B (s2(3). These are similar charges to those in class A.

c) Class C is subdivided as follows:

d) A puisne mortgage, i.e., a legal mortgage not being protected by the deposit of documents relating to the legal estate affected. a limited owner's charge, an equitable charge acquired by a tenant for life by a statutory owner by statute because he has paid taxes or other liability related to the estate.

 ii) A general equitable charge. This is a sweeping up charge, including all charges not protected by the deposit of title deeds etc.

iii) An estate contract. This is an estate contract by someone who is entitled at the date of contract to have the legal estate conveyed to him, to convey or create a legal estate.

d) Class D, this is a charge on land acquired by the commissioners of the Inland Revenue for unpaid capital transfer taxes.

e) Class E .This class covers annuities.

f) Class F covers charges affecting the matrimonial home by virtue of a spouses rights of occupation under the Matrimonial Homes Act 1983 as amended by the Family Law Act 1996.

Methods of making a land charges search

A search may be made in person, by post, or by telephone. Personal searches should not be made as this should be left to those who know the system and are employed to carry out searches.

A postal search effective for all registers is made on a form PIC. The information required for a postal search is the name of the estate owner, period of years searched against, address, county and description of property. Completed searches are usually sent back promptly. If the search reveals an adverse entry then the purchaser should ensure that the property concerned is not affected.

Other searches

Company searches are usually necessary if the property to be purchased is from a company. Company agents can ascertain whether there is a winding up order against the company or whether there are any specific charges relating to that company registered against the title to land.

The nature of the conveyance

It should be noted that if land to be conveyed is in an area of compulsory registration at the Land Registry, as most land is, the purchasers solicitor may, instead of preparing the traditional form of conveyance as described below, utilise the much simpler form of a registered land transfer. For more details concerning this form see chapter five. For those whose property will not be immediately registered the following applies.

The purchaser's solicitor will prepare a draft conveyance in duplicate and send it to the vendor's solicitor for scrutiny and approval. The vendor's solicitor will normally send back a copy with amendments in red pen. When the deed is agreed (settled) the purchaser's solicitor has it engrossed (fair copied) and then sends it to the vendor's solicitor to keep until the day of completion.

The contents of a typical conveyance of unregistered land

An example conveyance is shown further on in this chapter. The heading of the document will begin with the words "This conveyance" or "This deed of gift" etc. The conveyance is dated and the full names of the parties are inserted along with their addresses. If there are parties other than the vendor and purchaser, for example, any trustees, they are also inserted.

The Recital

This part of the deed will usually begin "whereas" and the purpose is to outline a history of transactions related to that property. They are largely unnecessary and are there as a result of tradition as it has evolved in conveyancing.

The Testatum

The testatum is part of the operative part of the conveyance and will begin with "Now this deed witnesses".

The formal words are followed by a statement of consideration for the transaction and a receipt by the vendor for the purchase money. No other receipt is required, although this does not stop a vendor challenging the fact that a receipt has been paid.

Words of grant

These are the words which pass the vendor's estate to the purchaser. The usual form of words will state "The vendor as beneficial owner hereby conveys". There will then be a description of the property conveyed, known as the parcels clause.

In a lease there will be what is known as a reddendum, which goes on to describe rent and rent days.

There are also what is known as covenants, either negative or positive covenants, which impose obligations, or rights on either party. In modern developments these conveyances are usually very lengthy and are contained in a schedule to the deed.

Where a vendor remains liable on a covenant after sale he or she should ensure that the purchaser enters into a covenant to indemnify the vendor in respect of any liability arising from a future breach of that covenant. The effect is to indemnify the vendor against any loss or expenses in respect of breach of covenant. Where the property is conveyed to joint tenants a clause is very often included declaring that each tenant holds joint equity and conferring on the co-owners additional powers of dealing with the land in question.

The testimonium

This is the formal clause, which precedes the party's execution of the deed and will typically be worded " In witness where of the parties here to have executed this document as their deed the day and year first before mentioned".

Execution of deeds before July 31st 1990

The Law of Property Act 1989 introduced very important changes in the execution of deeds. Under the Law of Property Act 1925 three formal requirements for a deed are outlined, namely that it must be signed sealed and delivered. The effective date of the deed is the effective date of delivery. However, after 1989 a seal is no longer required, just an effective signature, signed before a witness. The Companies Act 1989 also allows for companies to execute a deed by signature, with a seal no longer a requirement.

Completion of sale of unregistered land

The date for completion will be stated in the contract. See chapter 6. Usually, completion will take place at the offices of the vendor's solicitor. If there is an outstanding mortgage on the property and the mortgagee will not release the deeds to the vendors solicitor until after it is discharged then completion will take place at the mortgagees solicitor. Completion allows for settling of the financial account between vendor and purchaser and completion of legal work plus handing over the executed deed. Money is usually sent from a bank to the solicitor. Deeds are usually examined a last time to see that all is correct. The vendor may retain part of a title deed if there is any ongoing involvement, i.e., part ownership of land etc.

In unregistered conveyancing the legal estate is vested in the purchaser. The purchaser is also entitled to possession of the property and the solicitors should ensure that adequate arrangements have been made to this end.

Where the vendor is selling as a personal representative of another, a memoranda of sale should be endorsed on the grant of representation which he or she will have. Where the purchaser enters into covenants for the protection of land retained or is granted additional rights, such as rights over land, it is common for the vendor to retain a duplicate copy (counterpart).

Example of conveyance of unregistered land

This CONVEYANCE BY DEED is made the day of 20****
between J Smith of 19 Jupiter Street, Othertown (hereinafter called the vendor) of one part and F Deal of 1 Mars Street Eithertown (hereinafter called the purchaser) of the other part.
WHEREAS

(1) The vendor is seised of the property hereinafter described for an estate in fee simple in possession free from encumbrances and as hereinafter mentioned and has agreed with the purchaser for the sale to him of the said property for a like estate for a price of seventy five thousand pounds

NOW THIS DEED WITNESSETH

1._____ In pursuance of the said agreement and in consideration of the sum of <u>seventy five thousand pounds</u> now paid by the purchaser to the vendor (the receipt of which sum the vendor hereby acknowledges) the vendor as beneficial owner hereby conveys unto the purchaser all that land and property known as 41 Otherplace, Othertown as was conveyed to the vendor by John Rarer by a conveyance of 25th May 1952 and is further therein more particularly described and subject to the covenants therein contained but otherwise free from encumbrances <u>TO HOLD</u> the same unto the purchaser in fee simple_____

2. <u>With</u> the object and intent of affording to the vendor a full and sufficient indemnity but not further or otherwise the purchaser hereby covenants with the vendor to observe and perform the above mentioned covenant and to indemnify the vendor against all actions claims demands and liabilities in respect thereof _____

3. <u>It is hereby</u> certified that the transaction affected does not form part of a larger transaction or of a series of transactions in respect of which the amount or value or the aggregate amount or value of the consideration exceeds eighty pounds_____

___<u>IN WITNESS</u> whereof the parties hereto have executed this document as their deed the day and year first before written.

<u>EXECUTED AS HIS DEED</u>
By the aforementioned
J Smith in the presence of   ) J Smith

K Knowles   )
46 hilltop   )
Otherplace

EXECUTED AS HIS DEED

By the aforementioned
John Rarer in the presence of   ) John Rarer
K Smile   )
42 Child Street
Cidertown   )

Now read the key points from chapter four.

KEY POINTS FROM CHAPTER FOUR

- The purchasers solicitor will prepare a draft in conveyance in duplicate and send in duplicate to the vendors solicitor for scrutiny and approval.

- When the deal is agreed, the purchaser's solicitor has it engrossed and then sends it to the vendor's solicitor until completion.

- Deeds executed after July 31st 1990 do not require a seal.

- The date for completion should be clearly stated in the contract.

- Completion allows for the settling of the financial account between vendor and purchaser.

5

CONVEYANCING REGISTERED LAND – PROCESSES PRIOR TO COMPLETION

In chapter four, we looked at the general process of conveyancing unregistered land. In this chapter we will concentrate on registered land. In all likelihood, you will be dealing with registered land as most property is now registered.

First Registration of title

First registration of land may take place voluntarily or compulsorily depending on the nature of the transaction. Land Registry form FR1 should be used. Compulsory registration now extends to most of England and Wales. It is highly undesirable to complete a sale of land and then neglect to register it.

When a sale is completed an application must be lodged for registration within two months of completion. The effect of non-registration is that the deed of transfer, or the conveyance, becomes null and void after the two-month period. In other words, there is no choice but to register the land.

Under s123 of the Law of Property Act, the Chief Land Registrar may accept a late registration. An explanation of why the property was not registered within the time period will be required. Acceptance of the application has the effect of registering the estate to the purchaser from the date of completion. Late applications are rarely refused. When land is purchased in a compulsory area but the title is not yet registered, even where the transaction must be followed by a first registration the procedure until completion is identical to the procedure in unregistered conveyancing.

The purchaser's solicitor will forward the correct form to the land registry.

This form is called a "cover" because it is double sided and when folded will contain all the necessary documentation for registration. The cover will contain a certificate signed by a solicitor that the title has been properly investigated, a statement that any land charges entries revealed by the official search either do or do not affect the land concerned and if they do a note of the document by which they were created. In addition, a schedule of encumbrances affecting the property is sent.

All the original deeds and other documents of title must be sent. Enough information by way of plan must be sent to enable registry staff to fix the position of the property on the Ordnance Survey Map. There is a prescribed fee which the Land Registry can provide details of on request.

For application by the owner for first registration of leasehold land other than on the grant of a new lease and for application by the owner for first registration of leasehold land on grant of a new lease, see appendix for forms.

Outline of the Land Registry and the registration process

In registered land the documents of title are replaced by the fact of registration. Therefore, the equivalent to the title deed is the various entries in the Land Registry.

Each title is given a title number, which is then used to trace title.

The description of each title is identified by a title number, described by reference to a filed plan and a set of index cards retained to record specifics about that title.

The index cards and the filed plan are the equivalent of title deeds. The registered proprietor is issued with a land certificate containing a facsimile copy of the registered title. If land within a particular title number is subject to a mortgage the land certificate is retained by the Registry and the mortgagee is instead issued with a charge certificate, and the land certificate is retained by the Land Registry.

There are three registers of title at the Land Registry, the Property Register, The Proprietorship Register and the Charges Register.

The Property Register is similar to the Parcels Clause in unregistered conveyancing i.e. it describes the land in question. It will identify the geographical location and extent of the registered property by means of a short description and a reference to an official plan, which is prepared for each title. It may also give particulars of any rights that benefit the land, for example, a right of way over adjoining land. In the case of a lease the register will also describe the parties to the lease, the term and the rent, any exceptions or reservations from the lease and, if the lessors title is registered, the title number.

The Proprietorship Register is similar to the Habendum in unregistered conveyancing. It will describe the type of title, i.e., title absolute, leasehold etc, the full name and address of the registered proprietor, description of that person, date of registration, price paid for the property and any other relevant entries. There will also be any relevant cautions, inhibitions or restrictions entered on the Register.

The **Charges Register** contains any encumbrances affecting the registered property, such as mortgages and any other charges taken over the property. However, details of the amount of money involved are not disclosed.

How to inspect the Register

The Land Registry has an online conveyancing system. Normally, solicitors use this and evidence of title can be deduced by going into the web site. Evidence of title can also be obtained by writing to the Land Registry. If you wish, after you have received the copies of the register that you require, you can, by filling in the appropriate forms (see appendix 1) obtain copies of documents that you would like to inspect. Again, a fee is payable. If you only wish to know the name and address of the registered proprietor of a property, you should fill in Land Registry form PN1. You should then phone the Land Registry Customer Support Team on 0300 0441 or email at. customersupport@landregistry.gsi.gov.uk. They will direct you to the relevant office to send the form to.

The Land/Charge Certificate

Prior to 2003, when a title was registered for the first time or changed hands, a Land Certificate was issued by the Land Registry. The Land Certificate was regarded as the equivalent to the title deed although this can be misleading as it is only a facsimile of the official register and may not be up to date. In addition, there may be matters of title not contained on the register. The Land Certificate had to be produced to the appropriate Land Registry whenever there is a sale or transfer of land. A Charge Certificate had to be produced too.

As mentioned in the introduction, following the introduction of the Land Registration Act 2002, and the practice of 'dematerialisation' Land and Charge Certificates have now been abolished. If you have lost your certificate you do not need to replace it. Electronic copies of the land certificate can now be obtained through the Land Registry website.

Maps and descriptions of land

The Index map and parcels index provides that a map should be kept showing the position and extent of all registered titles. This is called the Public Index Map. This is open to inspection by any person, and can be inspected personally or by official search (see appendix). There will be a fee for this search.

All registered land must, in addition, be described by the applicant in such a way as to enable the land to be fully identified on the ordnance map or general map.

The Land Registry uses a consistent colour coding on its plans. This does not vary and it is expected that solicitors when preparing plans will use the same system. The colouring scheme is as follows:

- Red edging marks the extent of land within a particular title.
- Green tinting shows excluded pieces of land within the area of the title.
- Brown tinting shows land over which the registered land has a right of way.
- Blue tinting shows land within the title subject to a right of way.

For further references, colours are used in the following order:

a) Tinting in pink, blue yellow and mauve.

b) Edging with a blue yellow or mauve band.
c) Hatching with a colour other than black or green.
d) Numbering or lettering of small self contained areas.

In addition, when reading a filed plan it should be noted that a boundary represented by a feature shown on the ground or on the existing ordnance survey is represented by a continuous dark line. A boundary not representing such a feature is shown by a broken dark line.

The scale of the filed plan is usually 1/1250 enlarged from the survey 1/2500.

Now read the key points from chapter five.

****

KEY POINTS FROM CHAPTER FIVE

- Registered conveyancing entails the owner simply demonstrating that the registered proprietorship is recorded at the Land Registry.

- Each title is given a title number, which is described by reference to a filed plan and a set of Index Cards. These are the equivalent of title deeds

- There are three registers of title at the Land Registry, The Property Register, The Proprietorship Register and The Charges Register.

- The best and most convenient way of obtaining details from the Register is by post on Land Registry form number 109.

- First registration of land may take place voluntarily or be compulsory depending on the nature of the transaction.

THE CONTRACT FOR SALE –
EXCHANGE AND COMPLETION

6

THE CONTRACT FOR SALE

Forming the contract

Having discussed the processes involved in conveying registered and unregistered land, prior to exchange and completion, it is now necessary to look at the contract for sale, which is formulated at the outset but not exchanged or completed before all parties are satisfied with the prior processes of conveyancing.

As with many other transactions, a sale of land is effected through a contract. However, a contract, which deals with the sale of land, is governed by the requirements of the Law of Property (miscellaneous provisions) Act 1989, the equitable doctrine of specific performance and the duty of the vendor to provide title to the property.

The Law of Property Act (miscellaneous provisions) 1989 provides that contracts dealing with the sale of land after 26th September 1989 must be in writing. The contract must contain all the terms and agreements to which the respective parties to the transaction have agreed. The provisions of the Act do not apply to sales at a public auction, contracts to grant a short lease and contracts regulated under the Financial Services Act 1986. If the person purchasing is doing so through an agent then the agent must have authority to act on behalf of the purchaser. Examples of agents are auctioneers, solicitors and estate agents.

Agreements

If the phrase "subject to contract" is used in a sale then the intention of both parties to the contract is that neither are contractually bound until a formal contract has been agreed by the parties, signed and exchanged. Therefore, the words "subject to contract" are a protective device, although it is not good to depend on the use of these words throughout a transaction.

Procedures in the formation of contract

The vendor's solicitor will usually draw up an initial contract of sale. This is because only this person has access to all the necessary initial documents to begin to effect a contract. The draft contract is prepared in two parts and sent to the purchaser's solicitor (if using a solicitor) the other side will approve or amend the contract as necessary. Both sides must agree to any proposed amendments. (see standard letters used in process of conveyancing appendix 1). After agreement has been reached, the vendor's solicitor will retain one copy of the contract and send the other copy to the solicitor or person acting for the other side. The next stage is for the vendor's solicitor to engross (sign and formalise) the contract in two parts. Both parts are then sent to the purchaser's solicitor or other agent who checks that they are correct then sends one part back to the vendor's solicitor.

Signing the contract

The vendor's solicitor will obtain the vendor's signature to the contract, when he is satisfied that the vendor can sell what he is purporting to do through the contract. The purchaser's solicitor or agent will do the same, having checked the replies to all inquiries before contract. It is also essential to check that a mortgage offer has been made and accepted.

Signing the Transfer

The transfer (form TR1-see appendix) is the document transferring ownership of the property to the buyer. It confirms the details set out in the contract. The transfer is sent out by the solicitor (see standard letters appendix 1) for you to sign in readiness for exchange and completion.

Exchanging contracts

Neither party to the sale is legally bound until there has been an exchange of contracts. At one time, a face-to-face exchange would have taken place. However, with the rapid increases in property transactions this rarely happens nowadays. Exchange by post or telephone is more common. The purchaser will post his or her part of the contract together with the appropriate cheque, or bank transfer, to cover the agreed deposit to the purchaser's solicitor or person acting on behalf of that person. The deposit is usually 10% of the purchase price although there are variations on this theme. The amounts are agreed between buyer and seller. The purchaser's solicitor will usually insert the agreed completion date. On receiving this part of the contract the vendor will add his or her part and send this off in exchange. At this stage, both parties become bound under the contract.

The Contents of a contract

A contract will be in two parts, the particulars of sale and the conditions of sale. The particulars of sale give a physical description of the land and also of the interest which is being sold. A property must be described accurately and a plan may be attached to the contract to emphasise or illustrate what is in the contract. The particulars will also outline whether the property is freehold or leasehold and what kind of lease the vendor is assigning, i.e., head lease (where vendor is owner of the freehold) or underlease, (where the vendor is not).

It is very important to determine what kind of lease it is that is being assigned, indeed whether it is assignable or whether permission is needed from the landlord and it is recommended that a solicitor handle this transaction. This is because any purchaser of a lease can find his or her interest jeopardised by the nature of the lease. Where a sub-lease, or under lease is being purchased, the purchasers interest can be forfeited by the actions of the head lessee, the actions of this person being out of control of the purchaser.

Rights, such as easements and also restrictive covenants, which are for the benefit of the land, should be expressly referred to in the particulars of sale. In addition, the vendor should refer to any latent defects affecting his or her property, if known. This includes any encumbrances, which may affect the property.

Misdescription

If the property in the particulars of sale is described wrongly, i.e. there is a misstatement of fact, such as describing leasehold as freehold land, calling an under-lease a lease or leaving out something that misleads the buyer, in other words, if the mis description is material, then the purchaser is entitled to rescind the contract. Essentially the contract must describe what is being sold and if it does not, and the buyer is mislead then the contract is inaccurate.

If the misdescription is immaterial and insubstantial, and there has been no misrepresentation then the purchaser cannot rescind the contract. However, if the misdescription has affected the purchase price of the property then the purchaser can insist on a reduction in the asking price. The purchaser should claim this compensation before completion takes place.

The vendor has no right to rescind the contract if the misdescription is in the purchaser's favor, for example, the area of land sold is greater than that intended. Neither can the vendor compel the purchaser to pay an increased purchase price.

Misrepresentation

Misrepresentation is an untrue statement of fact made by one party or his or her agent, which induces the other party to enter into the contract. An opinion and a statement of intention must be distinguished from a statement of fact. There are three types of misrepresentation, fraudulent misrepresentation, negligent misrepresentation and innocent misrepresentation. Fraudulent misrepresentation is a false statement made knowingly or without belief in its truth, or recklessly. The innocent party may sue through the tort of negligence either before or after the contract is complete and rescind the contract. Negligent misrepresentation, although not fraudulent, is where the vendor or his or her agents cannot prove that the statement they made in relation to the contract was correct. Remedies available are damages or rescission of the contract. Innocent misrepresentation is where the statement made was neither fraudulently or negligently but is still an untrue statement. Rescission is available for this particular type of misrepresentation.

Rescission of contract generally is available under the Misrepresentation Act 1967 s 2(2).

Non-disclosure

Generally, in the law of contract, there is the principle of "caveat emptor" "let the buyer beware". In other words, it is up to the purchaser to ensure that what he or she is buying is worth the money paid for it. Earlier we talked about the importance of searches and also, particularly, the importance of the structural survey. Although the vendor has some responsibility to reveal any defects in the property it is always very advisable for the purchaser to ensure that all checks prior to purchase are carried out thoroughly.

Conditions of sale

There are two types of conditions, special conditions and general conditions. Special conditions are those which are specific to an individual contract, such as when a specific day is fixed for completion. The general conditions are those which have general application.

General conditions of sale are standard entitled, "National protocol for domestic leasehold and freehold property." This is a complete guide to conveyancing in itself and can be obtained from the Law Society. The Law Society has recently updated this protocol.

The general conditions of sale oblige the vendor to supply the purchaser with abstracts or any copies of a lease or agreement in writing. The vendor must always supply the purchaser with details of any tenancy agreements in existence. A deposit for the purchase will only be payable if there is a special or general condition to this effect, such a term is not implied into a contract. Under standard conditions a deposit of 10 percent of the purchase price is paid to the vendor's solicitor prior to purchase but this can be varied between parties. The deposit should be in cash or by banker's draft at the date of the contract (exchange). Failure to pay, or payment by a cheque, which is subsequently dishonored, is a breach and can lead to the vendor rescinding the contract. The general conditions specifically refer to this.

If there is any interest due, or expected on purchase money this will be dealt with in the special conditions of contract.

Completion

The requirements concerning completion are detailed thoroughly in the general conditions of sale. Payment on completion is one such detail. Payment on completion should be by one of the following methods:

- Legal tender.
- Bankers draft.
- An unconditional authority to release any deposit by the stakeholder.
- Any other method agreed with the vendor.

At common law, completion takes place whenever the vendor wishes and payment is to be made by legal tender.

Also dealt with in the general conditions is failure to complete and notices to complete. Failure to complete can cause difficulty for one of the other parties and the aggrieved party can serve notice on the other to complete by a specific date.

The notice has the effect of making "time of the essence" which means that a specific date is attached to completion, after which the contract is discharged.

Return of deposits

The vendor must return any deposit paid to the purchaser if the purchaser drops out before the exchange of contracts. This cannot be prevented and was the subject of a House of Lords ruling in the 1977 case Sorrel v Finch.

The position of the parties after exchange of contracts

Once a contract has been exchanged the purchaser is the beneficial owner of the property, with the vendor owning the property on trust for the purchaser. The vendor is entitled to any rents or other profits from the land during this period, and has the right to retain the property until final payments have been made and has a lien (charge/right) over the property in respect of any unpaid purchase monies.

The vendor is bound to take reasonable care of the property and should not let the property fall into disrepair or other damages to be caused during the period between exchange and completion. If completion does not take place at the allotted time and the fault is the purchasers then interest can be charged on the money due.

The purchaser, as beneficial owner of the property is entitled to any increase in the value of the land and buildings but not profits arising. The purchaser has a right of lien over the property, the same as the vendor, in respect of any part of the purchase price paid prior to completion.

Bankruptcy of the vendor

In the unfortunate event of the vendor going bankrupt in between exchange and completion, the normal principles of bankruptcy apply so that the trustee in bankruptcy steps in to the vendor's shoes. The purchaser can be compelled to complete the sale. The trustee in bankruptcy is obliged to complete the sale if the purchaser tenders the purchase money on the completion day.

Bankruptcy of the purchaser

When a purchaser is declared bankrupt in between sale and completion, all of his or her property vests in the trustee in bankruptcy. The trustee can compel the vendor to complete the transaction by paying monies due by the allotted day. If the vendor wishes to proceed with the sale and the trustee is reluctant, the trustee has the right to claim that the contract is onerous. However, in these circumstances, the vendor can keep any deposit due to him. A form for bankruptcy purchases is shown in appendix 1.

Death of the vendor or the purchaser

The personal representatives of a deceased vendor can compel the purchaser to sell. The money is conveyed to those representatives who will hold the money in accordance with the terms of any will or in accordance with the rules relating to intestacy if there is no will.

The same position applies to the purchaser's representatives, who can be compelled by the vendor to complete the purchase and who can hold money on the purchaser's behalf.

Other factors in the conveyancing process

Obtaining proof of identity

Solicitors are obliged by law to obtain evidence of those who intend to sell or purchase property. This is in line with regulations published in the Council of Mortgage Lenders Handbook-dealing with money laundering. The documents supplied (listed below) have to be certified either by a solicitor or the estate agent dealing with the sale. The post office can also verify the documents for a small fee.

You will need to prove identification and address.

Proof of identity

This can be your passport or photo card driving licence. A copy may be acceptable if it is certified as a true likeness by a regulated person.

Proof of address

This can be a utility bill less than three months old, a council tax demand or bank statement.

The solicitor in question will supply you with a list of acceptable documents.

Cash is not acceptable

Because of money laundering regulations, solicitors can only accept payments into bank accounts if they are from a UK bank or building society. If they are received from any other source then the solicitor is under an obligation to report the matter to the Serious Organized Crime Agency (SOCA).

Repaying a mortgage

If there is a mortgage on the property in question, this must be redeemed (paid off) on completion of the sale. Even if the mortgage is 'portable' then it still has to be paid off. A redemption statement has to be obtained from the lender, detailing the amount outstanding from that lender against that property. You should take into account any redemption penalties. The redemption statement is usually obtained at the beginning of the conveyance and then again at exchange of contracts.

Negative equity

If the amount to repay your mortgage is higher than the sale price contracts cannot be exchanged until any shortfall has been made up.

In virtually all cases, the mortgage is repaid in full on the day of completion by electronic transfer.

Now read the key points from chapter six.

****

KEY POINTS FROM CHAPTER SIX

- As with many other transactions, a sale of land is affected through a contract. The Law of Property Act, (Miscellaneous Provisions) 1988 provides that contracts dealing with the sale of land after 26th September 1989, must be in writing.

- If the phrase "subject to contract" is used then the intention of both parties to the contract is that neither are contractually bound until a formal contract has been agreed, signed and exchanged by the parties.

- Neither party is legally bound until there has been an exchange of contracts.

- Contracts are in two parts, The Particulars of Sale and the Conditions of Sale. The particulars give a physical description of the land and interest. There are two types of conditions, special and general. The latter is governed by the National Protocol for Domestic Leasehold and Freehold Property.

7

POST COMPLETION
REGISTERED AND
UNREGISTERED LAND

Completion of a land transaction will usually happen in the office of the vendor's solicitor. If there is an outstanding mortgage on the property and the mortgagee will not release the deeds until after payment has been made then completion will take place in the mortgagee's solicitors premises.

Completion will entail settling any outstanding payments between the vendor and purchaser. Also any legal work will be completed and deeds, if appropriate will be handed over.

On every transfer of sale of a freehold, lease or under-lease of seven years or more, the purchaser must complete a form giving particulars to the Inland Revenue. The form is to register the property for stamp duty and is known as "Stamps 1 (A) 451" or the "Particulars Delivered" form.

If the land is registered or being registered for the first time after completion, then if there is no stamp duty land tax (SDLT) payable the particulars must be sent to the Land Registry together with an application for registration. In every other case, the deed and the particulars delivered form must be sent to the Inland Revenue within thirty days of completion.

Stamp duty rates

Residential properties

The SDLT rates for residential properties changed on 4 December 2014. On 1st April 2016, the Stamp Duty Land Tax changed again, as all of those buying property as a second home or buy to let will incur an additional 3% stamp duty. The current rates and thresholds are shown below.

SDLT rates and thresholds for residential properties

SDLT is charged at increasing rates for each portion of the purchase price.

Property purchase price	SDLT rate from 4 December 2014
Up to £125,000	Zero
The next £125,000 (the portion from £125,001 to £250,000)	2%
The next £675,000 (the portion from £250,001 to £925,000)	5%
The next £575,000 (the portion from £925,001 to £1.5 million)	10%
The remaining amount (the portion above £1.5 million)	12%
All properties as buy to let or second home	additional 3%

Residential leaseholds

If you buy a new residential leasehold, SDLT is payable on both the:

- purchase price (lease premium) - use the current SDLT residential rates

- 'net present value' (NPV) of the rent payable

The NPV is based on the value of the total rent over the life of the lease.

NPV of rent (residential)	SDLT rate
£0 to £125,000	Zero
The portion over £125,000	1%

Corporate bodies

SDLT is charged at 15% on residential properties costing more than £500,000 bought by certain corporate bodies (or 'non-natural persons'). These include:

- companies

- partnerships including companies

- collective investment schemes

The 15% rate doesn't apply to property bought by trustees of a settlement or bought by a company to be used for:

- a property rental business

- property developers and trader

- property made available to the public

- financial institutions acquiring property in the course of lending

- property occupied by employees

- farmhouses

The standard residential rate of SDLT applies in these cases. These exclusions are subject to specific conditions.

Buying 6 or more residential properties in one transaction

If 6 or more properties form part of a single transaction the rules, rates and thresholds for non-residential properties apply.

The amounts paid for all the properties in the transaction must be added together to establish the SDLT payable.

Non-residential and mixed use properties

Non-residential property includes:

- commercial property such as shops or offices

- agricultural land

- forests

- any other land or property which is not used as a dwelling

- 6 or more residential properties bought in a single transaction

A mixed use property is one that incorporates both residential and non-residential elements.

SDLT rates and thresholds for sales and transfers on new non-residential or mixed use land or property

The rates below apply to freehold and leasehold non-residential and mixed use purchases and transfers.

Purchase price/lease premium or transfer value	SDLT rate
Up to £150,000 - if annual rent is under £1,000	Zero
Up to £150,000 - if annual rent is £1,000 or more	1%
£150,001 to £250,000	1%
£250,001 to £500,000	3%
Over £500,000	4%

The annual rent is the highest annual rent known to be payable in any year of the lease, not the NPV used to determine any tax payable on the rent.

SDLT rates and thresholds for rent on new non-residential or mixed use land or property

If you buy a new non-residential or mixed use leasehold property, SDLT is payable on both the:

- lease premium or purchase price

- NPV of the rent payable

These are calculated separately and then added together.

NPV of rent	SDLT rate

NPV of rent	SDLT rate
£0 - £150,000	Zero
The portion of the value over £150,000	1%

An application must be made to the Land Registry to register the transaction. This will involve sending:

1. The fee
2. The transfer form TR1 which is used in all cases where the transfer of a title has happened.
3. Evidence of any previous mortgage being paid off.
4. Details of the new charge by the delivery of a copy of the mortgage and original mortgage.

The title can then be registered in the name of the new purchaser together with details of any new charge.

Once registration is complete a copy should be sent to the purchaser for checking and any original documents should be sent to the lender for safekeeping.

****

CONCLUSION

This book is intended to be a guide to the processes of conveyancing and should be used in conjunction with a solicitor.

The book is very much about the procedures involved in buying and selling property. However, unless a conveyance is likely to be straightforward then you are advised to employ a solicitor or licensed conveyancer to carry out the work. Prices for such work are quite often very competitive and if there is a problem along the way then at least you have redress after the event.

Summary of process

We saw in chapter two that there are basic searches common to all properties that must be carried out prior to exchange of contracts. In chapter three we discussed the importance of carrying out a structural survey before committing to a purchase. In chapter four we discussed the various issues concerning unregistered land and the need to prove title and to carry out further additional searches. In chapter five we discussed the issues surrounding registered land and proof of title. Finally we discussed the contract for sale and process of completion following the various stages of conveyancing of land. Standard letters relating to each of these stages are contained within appendix 1. The standard forms used are contained within appendix 2.

A few simple words of advice:

When buying property make sure that all debts are paid by the vendor before completing. This is especially pertinent to leasehold property that is quite often subject to a service charge. If the vendor does not settle debts then the purchaser will find his or herself taking on the debt. Read contracts/leases very carefully indeed. Make sure that you know what it is that you are buying and that you are fully aware. Buying and selling property is a complex task-be very cautious and always scrutinise all documents very carefully. Make sure that what you buy is in sound condition and represents a good investment. It is the biggest investment that you will probably make.

****

Glossary

A

Acting for both parties

There are limited circumstances when solicitors can act for both parties

Amount outstanding on the mortgage

Also known as the redemption figure

Apportionment of the purchase price

This may be used to save stamp duty land tax Fixtures and fittings known as chattels do not attract stamp duty and this is why the distinction between those and land is important.

Attorneys

A deed may be signed by an attorney but evidence of his power of attorney must be produced as this will be required by the land registry.

Auctions

The auction contract is usually prepared in advance The purchaser has the right to undertake all his searches en enquiries and survey before the auction. Once the auction has been concluded usually a ten per cent deposit is taken and the sale takes place 28 days later. It would be necessary for anyone entering into an auction to have their finance in place before the hammer falls.

B

Boundaries

Even with a registered title the boundaries shown on the filed plan are general boundaries and are not definitive. The rule is generally what has been there for the last 12 years is the boundary this may have to be supported by statutory declarations.

Breach of a Restrictive Covenant

Or other defect.

Indemnity insurance might be available

Bridging Finance

This might be for a deposit which is repaid on the sale of the property. It is rare for English banks to extend finance for a property that is open ended. It is usually only extended once contracts are exchange and there is a fixed date for completion.

Building Regulation Consent

This may be required even if there are not developments that require planning permission. It relates to health and safety matters and the type of materials used on completion of building works for which consent it required a final certificate must be obtained from the local authority. This is evidence that the building regulations have been complied with.

C

Capital Gains Tax

The main exemption which affects residential conveyancing is the principal private dwelling house exemption The seller must have occupied the dwelling house as his only or main residence throughout the period of ownership There is a sliding scale for absences and exemptions of short periods of absence

Capacity

The seller might be sole owner, joint owner, personal representative mortgagee, charity, company bankrupt or otherwise incapacitated.

Classes of Title

There are different classes of title the best being absolute title but there is also possessory title qualified title and good leasehold title

Contaminated Land

Any contamination could have serious effects in that it may be impossible to sell or obtain a mortgage on.

Completion

The day on which the transaction is finalised, the money changes hands and the parties vacate and take possession of the land that is the moving day.

Co-Ownership

This is where more than one person owns the land such as tenant in common or joint tenant.

Conveyancing

The process of transferring the ownership of freehold and leasehold land.

Compulsory Registration

This has arisen since 1990 and applies to the whole of England and Wales. The categories of events triggering a registration have changed but it is still not compulsory to register land without one of these triggers but voluntary registration could take place.

Conservation Area

Any non listed building in a conservation area must not be demolished with conservation area consent. There are also restrictions on development.

Contract Races

This is where more than one contract has been issued solicitors are obliged to let both parties know the terms of the race that is what needs to be done to secure the property. It must be confirmed in writing. A standard contact race would specific that the first person to be in a position to exchange contracts unconditionally wins the race. This is usually signified by the purchasers solicitors producing a signed contract and deposit together with authority to proceed.

Covenants

This is a promise made in a deed and binding any subsequent owner of the land they may include such matter as maintaining the fences and only using the land for the erection of one property.

D

Deeds

Apart from unregistered land most deeds have now dematerialised as they are registered at the land registry. Evidence of ownership is shown by official copies of the registered entries. This is an official dated document showing the current state of the title.

Deposit

Although not a legal requirement is it customary and it's a form of security and part payment towards the purchase price.

Discharge of seller's mortgage

On completion is the seller has a mortgage this will need to be paid off and evidence given to the purchasers solicitor. This will need to be lodged at the land registry as proof of the discharge before a new purchaser can be substituted and maybe a new mortgage started.

Draft contract

The name attached to the contract before it is agreed by the parties and prior to exchange of contracts. Once the contract is approved it can be signed by the parties and forms the basis of the transactions. They must be in the same format. Identical contracts are exchanged.

E

Easements

This is a right over land of another such as a right of way or of light.

Engrossment

Merely means s properly types up version of a document the draft is amended then the engrossment is the fair copy

Escrow

A document such as contract mortgage transfer is delivered and will not become effective until some future date. It is therefore held in escrow the condition being that the event takes place such as completion or exchange of contracts. Gets rid of the need for all the parties to a transaction being in the same room at the same time.

Exchange of contracts

When the parties agree to bind themselves legally to buy and sell the land.

Execution

Means the signing of a document in a certain way for a deed to be valid it must contain the words this deed signed by the necessary parties in the presence of a witness and be delivered.

F

Filed plan

In conveyancing a plan is a map showing the land referred to edged in red. It is the official designation of the land for land registry purposes

Fixture and fittings

Now a formal part of the process in that purchasers solicitor will expect to see a completed fixtures and fittings form. It may be acceptable to apportion part of the price for fixtures and fittings and this is sometimes undertaken when the price falls on one of the bands for change in stamp duty. The list must be legitimate ad the revenue have the right to query this and levy any tax not paid

Fixtures and fittings distinction

Between objects not attached to the land are fittings and those attached are fixtures. The current fixtures and fitting list covers most eventualities but care should be taken if an offer is deemed to include items at the property they should be specifically mentioned in the

Full Survey

As the name suggests this is full survey of the property and should contain a detailed breakdown of every aspect of the property.

H

Home Buyers Valuation and Survey Report

This is a compromise between a full structural survey and valuation.

I

Insurance

The risk on the property passes when contracts are exchanged. Even thought he purchaser has not got possession. The property is usually also insured by the seller up until the date of completion. They both have an insurable risk.

Indemnity Covenants

Any owner of land will remain liable for the covenants and passes these on by way of an indemnity covenant by any incoming purchaser

Investigating Title

Once the seller has produced the contract package the purchasers solicitors investigate title. This is to ensure that the seller is the owner of the property which is the subject of the contract. Also it must not reveal any defects other than those can be rectified prior to exchange of contracts.

There may for instance be consent required from a third party such as the necessity to register the transfer of a lease and become the member of a management company.

J

Joint tenants

This is most common between husband and wife. Both own equal shares in the property if either were to die the other inherit by way of survivorship. They cannot leave their share by will to anyone else.

L

Listed Building

Where a building might be of outstanding historic or architectural important the secretary of state may list it. Any alterations to the property will require both planning permission and listed building consent.

M

Mortgage

Is where the owner of land borrows money on the security of the land Also known as a legal charge. The lender has certain statutory powers the most important being that they can sell the property in the event of the loan not being paid.

Mortgage Fraud

Normally some proof of identity is required but this has been overtaken by the money laundering rules whereby it is accepted practice that clients should produce to their solicitors all the usual forms of ID to include utility bills driving licence passport etc.

Mortgages Repayments

The main types of repayment are pension, endowment and interest only. They do not affect the conveyancing transaction but some may have slightly different procedures between the conveyancers and the lender such as notices or deposit of insurance policies.

O

Occupiers Rights

The most important is the spouse of the seller. They have a statutory right to occupy the matrimonial home. Usually an enquiry is made as to there being any other occupiers of the matrimonial home. They are then asked to sign the contract to confirm they will give vacant possession completion.

Office Copy Entries

Usually refers to the registered title but can relate to any official copy issued by the land or other registries. They are acceptable as the originals.

Overriding Interests

These are matters affecting the land which are not on the register although this is being resolved under the current land registry rules. The most important being rights of way not mentioned on the deeds local land charges squatters rights.

P

Planning - Use of the property

It should be checked that the property has permission for its current use. Any purchaser should be aware that any change of use form its current use may require planning permission. For example a residential property may not be used for the fixing and selling of cars without a change of use. Any breach will be enforced by the local planning authority.

Planning Breach

This could be rectified by retrospective permission or again by indemnity insurance.

Purchase Deed

Now the transfer or TR1 this is the document that is signed by the seller transferring the land from the seller to the purchaser. It is signed prior to completion and once the formalities have been finalised such as the passing of the money it will be forwarded to the purchasers solicitors. This document will need to be stamped and registered at the land registry.

Possessory Title

The registry may grant a possessory title in the event of lack of paper title and eventually it can be upgraded to an absolute title. Land can be acquired through adverse possession but it is still subject to all covenants and easements etc existing at the date of the registration

Post Contact Stage

Between exchange of contracts and completion essential things such as finance is resolved as our final searches and all documents signed in readiness for completion.

R

Radon

If the property is in an area affected by radon gas a specific search should be undertaken which will reveal whether a survey has been undertaken and remedial measures have been taken.

Registered land

A state run system that proves the ownership of land by have a title registered at the HM land registry.

S

Searches

There are a series of searches. Before exchange of contracts the local authority search, after exchange bankruptcy and land registry searches.

Special Conditions

Any special condition will be used to vary the standard conditions of sale contained in the contract

Subject to Contract

This is of historical interest now as it is not possible to exchange contracts inadvertently or entering into irrevocably buying land without a proper contract. Some organisations still insist on using it as it gives them comfort Not now necessary in view of the Law Of Property (Miscellaneous) Provisions act 1989

Survey

There are many kinds of survey form the mere valuation by a lender to a full structural survey. Any purchaser should be aware that at the moment the law says *caveat emptor* that is let the buyer beware. Apart form a deliberate misstatement the seller is not liable for the current state of the property. An invariable practice is for purchasers to be advised to have a survey of the property and not to rely solely on the building society valuation.

Title

Either the registered or unregistered proof of the seller's ownership of the land.

Title Number

Every piece of registered land has a unique title number and must be used in all official documents searches etc.

Tenants in Common

Is where two or more people own land jointly in separate shares. Either owner can pass their share by will to anyone they wish.

Tenure

The legal term for how the land is being held being either freehold or leasehold.

U

Unregistered Land

The seller has to prove title by a series of documents such as conveyances, mortgagees etc now being replaced by registered conveyancing.

Undertakings

These are promises by solicitor to undertake certain acts. The most common being that the sellers solicitor will discharge the existing mortgage. Failure to comply with the undertaking is a professional offence so therefore they will not be entered into lightly and can be relied up They should always be confirmed in writing and their terms made certain.

Upgrading Title

Either on application or on the initiative of the registrar a title may be upgraded such as possessory to absolute and the same for qualified and good leasehold title

V

Valuation

Can either be an estate agents valuation which is a financial matter for the purchasers and sellers a lenders valuation is the figure that is used to calculate how much the lender is prepared to lend. This is based on a valuers report prepared for the lender once the buyer has requested a loan. It is an assessment of the value not a survey of the property. Lenders will normally exclude liability for any defects in the property. They are not undertaking that the property is fit for its purpose just because they are prepared to lend on it.

Value Added Tax – VAT

Is payable on solicitors costs but not o the purchase price of second hand properties. There is not VAT payable on stamp duty or land registry fees in a domestic transaction.

W

Witnesses

Must be a responsible adult and is usually independent of the parties who must add name, address and occupation

STANDARD LETTERS

SALE OF PROPERTY
First Letter to Purchaser's Solicitors

3 April, 2016

Address

Dear Sirs

Re   Property:
      Your Client:
      Our Client:

We understand that you act on behalf of ??????? of ???????????? in connection with their proposed purchase of the above from our clients ?????????????.

We would be obliged if you could confirm that if your clients have a property to sell a purchaser has been found and if your client should require finance this has been approved at least in principle.

Subject to the above being confirmed we will arrange for a draft Contract to be issued to you as soon as possible.

Yours faithfully

Letter to Building Society / Bank Requesting Title Deeds

3 April, 2016

Address

Dear Sirs

Re   Property:
       Account Number:
       Borrower:

We act for the above named clients in connection with the sale of the above property and we shall be obliged if you would please send us have the Title Deeds relating to this property.

We undertake to hold them to your order pending redemption of the mortgage.

At the same time please let us know the amount owing under this mortgage.

Yours faithfully

Authority to Bank to Obtain Title Deeds

3 April, 2016

Address

Dear Sirs

We hereby give you authority to release the Title Deeds for property listed below to …………….. of ……………..

Address of Property: …………………………………….

Address of Lender: …………………………………….

Account Number: …………………………………….

Signature …………………………………….

Letter Issuing Contract etc to Purchaser's Solicitors

3 April, 2016

Address

Dear Sirs

Re   Property:
        Your Client:
        Our Client:

Thank you for your letter of ????????. We take this opportunity of enclosing:

1. Draft Contract in duplicate

2. Official Copy of Register Entries plus File Plan

3. Fixtures Fittings and Contents List

4. Seller's Property Information Form

5. Copy Transfer dated ??????????

Yours faithfully

Letter Sending Approved TR1 and Replies to Requisitions on Title

3 April, 2016

Address

Dear Sirs

Re   Property:
        Your Client:
        Our Client:

Thank you for your letter of .... we take this opportunity of enclosing the following:

1. TR1 approved as amended

2. Requisitions on Title and our replies thereto

Yours faithfully

Letter to Purchaser's Solicitor on Exchange of Contracts

3 April, 2016
Fax & Post
Fax Number:

Address

Dear Sirs

Re   Property:
           Your Client:
           Our Client:

Further to our telephone conversation at 2:15 p.m. between ......
and .... Contracts were exchanged and the date fixed for
completion is ....

The sale price is £....... and you will be holding the £........ deposit
strictly to our order pending completion.

We enclose our client's part of the Contract to complete exchange of
Contracts. .

Yours faithfully

Letter to Bank/Building Society Requesting Redemption Figure

3 April, 2016

Building Society
Address

Dear Sirs

Re: Borrower:
        Property:
        Account No:

Would you please let us have the redemption figure on the above mortgage account as at *date.......*

Yours faithfully

Index

Appendix 1 Sample conveyancing costs 2 bed freehold House

PURCHASE STATEMENT FEBRUARY 2016 FOR FREEHOLD HOUSE	Using Licensed conveyancers.		
Our fees for	£ (net)	£ (VAT)	£ (Gross)
Purchase Conveyance	349.00	69.80	418.80
Preparation of the Stamp Duty Land	85.00	17.00	102.00
Transaction Return			
Money Laundering check (per customer	17.00	3.40	20.40
Professional Fee-Access online searches and Land Registry documentation	39.69	7.94	47.63
Local Search	125.00	25.00	150.00
Drainage Search	41.32	8.26	49.58
Environment Search	45.80	9.16	54,96
Bankruptcy Search	2.50	0.50	3.00
Land Registry Priority Search	4.50	0.90	5.40

Preparation of the Chancel Repair Indemnity Insurance*	17.00	3.40	20.40
Archive of documents associated with your purchase**	25.00	5.00	30.00
Total	751.81	150.36	902.17

Based on the information we have at present, the following fees may also be applicable on your transaction.

Our fees for	£ (net)	£ (VAT)	£ (Gross)
Acting for your lender for each Mortgage***(payable by you in accordance with your mortgage conditions)	150.00	30.00	180.00
Each electronic payment by CHAPS	40.00	8.00	48.00
Each electronic payment by BACS	8.50	1.70	10.20
Payments to third parties, including Government Agencies			
H.M. Land Registry charges			70.00
Government Stamp Duty			0.00
Chancel Repair Liability Indemnity Premium (inc of insurance premium tax) *			5.25
total			313.45
Overall Total			1,215,62

If there is an existing Home Information Pack with acceptable searches the Local Search Fee and Drainage Search Fee will not apply.

For other locality searches that may be required, e. g. coal search or tin search see our menu of additional services.

If the property is Leasehold, there will be additional third party payments.

- Subject to change if the purchase property cannot be covered by the Block Chancel Repair Indemnity Policy proposed. Please refer to Fact Sheet enclosed for those exceptions. If the property is an excepted case a policy may still be obtainable and we will contact you during the transaction if this is the case.
- There will be no further charge if you require retrieval of your documents in the future. Please note the charge is £25.00 plus VAT for a single transaction. A combined fee of £30.00 plus VAT will be charged for this service if a related transaction is instructed.*** If a second mortgage, other charge or secured loan is to be taken out on the property, an additional legal fee for acting for your lender plus VAT will be payable for each additional one.

Appendix 2

SAMPLE OF DOCUMENTS TO BE USED IN CONVEYANCING SHOWN OVERLEAF

1)   PROTOCOL FORMS

    a)   Fixtures, Fittings and Contents (4th Edition)

    b)   Sellers Property Information Form (4th Edition)

    c)   Sellers Leasehold Information Form (3rd Edition)

2)   General Leasehold Enquiries

Property:	
Seller:	

These enquiries are asked on behalf of buyers. The Seller should only respond to these enquiries if they are the Landlord, the Management Company, the Managing Agent or the Residents' or Tenants' Association or are representing any of them.

TERM	DEFINITION
Ground Rent	The rent payable to the landlord by the lessee as required by the lease.
HMO	A House in Multiple Occupation as defined by section 257 of the Housing Act 2004.
Landlord	The person or company which has granted a lease over the Property to the owner of the Property.
Lessees	The owners of properties in the Managed Area.
Managed Area	The properties including the building containing the Property, together with any land, managed by or on behalf of the Landlord under the terms of the lease. Managed Areas are sometimes also called common parts.
Management Company	A management company referred to in the lease, or a Right to Manage Company created under the Commonhold & Leasehold Reform Act 2002, to provide services and administer the terms of the lease either directly or through managing agents.
Managing Agent	A person or organisation which acts on behalf of the landlord, management company or Right to Manage Company [within their terms of reference, subject to any legal restrictions].
Property	The property known by the above address, including any land and outbuildings leased to the Seller.
Reserve Fund	A fund collected from the Lessees which allows the build-up of monies to pay for repairs and the replacement of major items (such as lifts) or to equalise cyclical expenditure (such as external decoration), avoiding excessive peaks in the Service Charge. Reference to Reserve Fund includes any sinking fund or replacement fund.
Residents'/Tenants' Association	A group of some or all of the Lessees with or without a formal constitution or corporate status, or a recognised residents association which is 'recognised' by law and with a formal constitution.
Right to Manage Company	A company owned by the Lessees that manages the Managed Areas on behalf of the Landlord or Management Company, within their terms of reference, subject to any limitations.
Service Charge	The amount payable by a lessee as a contribution to the costs of services, repairs, maintenance, insurance, improvements or costs of management etc. as set out in the lease. The amount payable may vary according to the costs incurred or to be incurred.
Section 20	Section 20 of the Landlord & Tenant Act 1985, which requires the Landlord or Managing Agents to consult with the Lessees about certain proposed works.

Please complete the information requested. It is important that the incoming lessee is fully aware of their obligation so the information given must be as accurate as possible. If there is insufficient space, continue on a separate sheet.

SECTION 1: CONTACT DETAILS		Complete the details for the relevant parties or cross through if not applicable. If there are more parties involved, provide details on a separate sheet.
1.1 Landlord	**1.2**	**Management Company**
Name Address Telephone Email	Name Address Telephone Email	
1.3 Managing Agent	**1.4**	**Residents'/Tenants' Association**
Name Address Telephone Email Appointed by: ☐ Management Company ☐ Landlord ☐ Other	Name Address Telephone Email	

1.5 Who accepts service of the Notice of Assignment & Charge?

Tick the box beside each party and state the total fee including VAT for notice of assignment and charge.

☐ Landlord   £ _____
☐ Management Company   £ _____
☐ Managing Agent   £ _____
☐ Other   £ _____

If other, provide contact details for service:

Name [ ]

Address [ ]

Telephone [ ]

Email [ ]

Capacity (e.g. Landlord's lawyer) [ ]

1.6 Who collects the Ground Rent?

☐ Landlord   ☐ Management Company   ☐ Managing Agent   ☐ N/A

1.7 Who collects the Service Charges?

☐ Landlord   ☐ Management Company   ☐ Managing Agent   ☐ N/A

1.8   Who collects the building insurance premiums?

☐ Landlord   ☐ Management Company   ☐ Managing Agent   ☐ N/A

1.9   Who deals with the day to day maintenance of the building?

☐ Landlord   ☐ Management Company   ☐ Managing Agent   ☐ the Lessees

1.10   Who deals with the day to day maintenance of the Managed Area?

☐ Landlord   ☐ Management Company   ☐ Managing Agent   ☐ the Lessees   ☐ N/A

1.11   Who organises and administers the buildings insurance?

☐ Landlord   ☐ Management Company   ☐ Managing Agent   ☐ the Lessees   ☐ N/A

SECTION 2: TRANSFER & REGISTRATION

2.1   Is a Deed of Covenant required?   ☐ Yes   ☐ No   ☐ Not Known

2.1.1   If Yes, confirm the costs applicable to the Deed including VAT   £ _____

2.2   Is a Licence to Assign required?   ☐ Yes   ☐ No

2.3   If Yes, specify requirements e.g. references, and any costs applicable to the Licence:

2.4   Are you aware of consent having been given to any alterations or additions to the Property?   ☐ Yes   ☐ No

2.4.1   If Yes, provide details and copies of any consent:

2.5   Is the incoming Lessee required to take a share in, or become a member of, the Management Company?   ☐ Yes   ☐ No   ☐ N/A

2.5.1   If Yes, provide details of the procedure and fees:

2.6   What is the procedure and cost for obtaining a certificate in accordance with a restriction in the Proprietorship Register at the Land Registry, if applicable?

SECTION 3: GROUND RENT

3.1   What is the annual Ground Rent payable for the Property?   £ _____

3.2   Is the Ground Rent paid up to date?   ☐ Yes   ☐ No

3.2.1   If No, supply details of the arrears:

3.3   What period is covered by the last demand?   From: __ / __ / _____ To: __ / __ / ____

SECTION 4: SERVICE CHARGE

4.1   How many properties contribute toward the maintenance of the Managed Area?

4.1.1   What is the current annual Service Charge for the Property?   £ _____

4.2   Is the Service Charge paid up to date for the Property?   ☐ Yes   ☐ No

4.2.1   If No, supply details of the arrears:

4.3   Is any excess payment anticipated for the Property at the end of the financial year?   ☐ Yes   ☐ No

4.3.1   If Yes, provide details:

4.4   What period is covered by the last demand?   From: __ / __ / _____ To: __ / __ / ____

4.5   In the last 12 months, has any inability to collect payments, from any party, affected (or is it likely to affect), the maintenance of the Managed Area?   ☐ Yes   ☐ No

4.5.1   If Yes, provide details:

4.6   Does a Reserve Fund apply to the Managed Area?   ☐ Yes   ☐ No

4.6.1   If Yes, confirm the amount collected from Lessees of the Property, currently held in the Reserve Fund: £ _____

4.6.2   Is the amount expected to be sufficient to cover the known Section 20 expenditure?   ☐ Yes   ☐ No

4.6.3   If No, supply details:

4.7   Confirm the date when the Managed Areas were last decorated, internally and externally.   Internally Date: __ / __ / ____ To: __ / __ / ____

Externally Date: __ / __ / ____ To: __ / __ / ____

4.8   Within the next 2 years, are any Section 20 works proposed to the Property?   ☐ completed but unpaid

☐ due

☐ anticipated

☐ N/A

4.8.1   If so, provide details of the works and the contribution anticipated from the Lessee:

4.9   Is any increase in the Service Charge over 10% or £100, whichever is the greater, anticipated in the next 2 years?   ☐ Yes   ☐ No

4.9.1   If Yes, provide details:

4.10   Are there any outstanding Service Charge consultation procedures?   ☐ Yes   ☐ No

4.10.1   If Yes, provide details:

4.11   Are the Managed Areas known to be affected by Japanese knotweed?   ☐ Yes   ☐ No

4.11.1   If Yes, provide details and a copy of any Japanese knotweed management plan in place.

4.12   Are there any: ☐ Yes   ☐ No
-transfer fees,
-deferred service charges or
-similar fees
expressed as a percentage of the Property's value payable on an event such as resale or subletting?

4.12.1   If Yes, provide details:

SECTION 5: BUILDINGS INSURANCE

5.1   Are the buildings insurance premium contributions paid up to date for the Managed Areas including the Property?   ☐ Yes   ☐ No

5.1.1   If No, provide details of the arrears:

5.2   What period is covered by the last demand?   From: __ / __ / _____   To: __ / __ / _____

5.3   Has the premium been paid in full?   ☐ Yes   ☐ No

5.3.1   If No, provide details:

5.4   Have any claims been made against the policy during the last 3 years?   ☐ Yes   ☐ No   ☐ Not Known

5.4.1   If Yes, provide details:

5.5   Are any claims anticipated?   ☐ Yes   ☐ No

5.5.1   If Yes, provide details:

5.6   Are the Managed Areas covered by the policy?   ☐ Yes   ☐ No

5.6.1   (i) Has a fire risk assessment been completed?   ☐ Yes   ☐ No   ☐ No common parts

    (ii) Have any works recommended been carried out?   ☐ Yes   ☐ No   ☐ N/A

5.6.2   If No to either of the above, has the insurer been made aware of this and accepted the position?   ☐ Yes   ☐ No

5.7 Please confirm the date of the last buildings reinstatement ___ / ___ / _____
cost assessment.

5.8 Is the insurance premium included in the service charge ☐ Yes ☐ No
budget?

5.8.1 If No, confirm the annual amount payable for the Property: £ _____

SECTION 6: DISPUTES & ENFRANCHISEMENT

6.1 Are there any on-going forfeiture proceedings in relation ☐ Yes ☐ No
to the Property?

6.2 Are there any documented unresolved disputes with the ☐ Yes ☐ No
Lessees of any of the properties in the Managed Area?

6.2.1 If Yes, to the extent permitted by the Data Protection Act
1998, please supply details:

6.3 Have any steps been taken by anyone to enfranchise, ☐ Yes ☐ No ☐ Not Known
exercise the right to manage, form a right to enfranchise
or management company, extend the term of the lease of
the Property or anything similar?

6.3.1 If Yes, provide details and copies of relevant
documentation:

6.4 Are you aware of any breach of the terms of the lease of ☐ Yes ☐ No
this Property?

6.4.1 If Yes, provide details:

SECTION 7: GENERAL

7.1 How many other properties are there in the Managed _____
Area?

7.2 Are they all leased on leases with similar terms? ☐ Yes ☐ No ☐ Not Known

7.2.1 If No, provide details:

7.3 Is the building in which the Property is situated known to ☐ Yes ☐ No ☐ Not Known
be an HMO?

7.3.1 If Yes, confirm that regulations applicable to section
257 Housing Act 2004 HMOs have been complied with:

SECTION 8: REQUIRED DOCUMENTS

Please provide the following applicable documents:-

8.1 The last 3 years published Service Charge accounts: ☐ Enclosed ☐ To follow ☐ N/A

8.2 Buildings insurance policy and schedule: ☐ Enclosed ☐ To follow ☐ N/A

8.3 Buildings insurance policy and schedule for the Managed ☐ Enclosed ☐ To follow ☐ N/A
Areas:

8.4	Service charge estimate for the current year and details of the anticipated payments on account for the Property:	☐ Enclosed	☐ To follow	☐ N/A
8.5	Service charge estimate for the previous year for which accounts have not yet been prepared for the Property:	☐ Enclosed	☐ To follow	☐ N/A
8.6	Copies of any notices served on the Lessees under Section 20 in respect of any proposed works or any works which have not yet been paid for:	☐ Enclosed	☐ To follow	☐ N/A
8.7	Documentation relating to any forfeiture proceedings applicable to the Property:	☐ Enclosed	☐ To follow	☐ N/A
8.8	Any additional regulations or rules affecting the Property which are not contained in the lease:	☐ Enclosed	☐ To follow	☐ N/A

8.9 Any Deeds of Variation or other document varying the terms of the lease of this Property:

☐ Enclosed ☐ To follow

☐ Landlord's lawyer provides

☐ Please supply draft ☐ N/A

8.10 Any required Deed of Covenant:

☐ Enclosed ☐ To follow

☐ Landlord's lawyer provides

☐ Please supply draft ☐ N/A

8.11 Any Certificate of Compliance:

☐ Enclosed ☐ To follow

☐ Landlord's lawyer provides

☐ Please supply draft ☐ N/A

8.12 Any required Licence to Assign:

☐ Enclosed ☐ To follow

☐ Landlord's lawyer provides

☐ Please supply draft ☐ N/A

8.13	Copy of any permission to alter the Property which has been issued:	☐ Enclosed	☐ To follow	☐ N/A
8.14	Copy of any known notices served on the Lessee and documentation arising from them:	☐ Enclosed	☐ To follow	☐ N/A
8.15	Asbestos Survey for parts of the Managed Area built or converted before 2001:	☐ Enclosed	☐ To follow	☐ N/A
8.16	Fire Risk Assessment for the Managed Area:	☐ Enclosed	☐ To follow	☐ N/A
8.17	Memorandum and Articles of Association of the Management Company:	☐ Enclosed	☐ To follow	☐ N/A
8.18	Minutes of the last AGM for the Management Company:	☐ Enclosed	☐ To follow	☐ N/A

Second Edition 2015

Signed	Dated ....
Print Name: .... Company:	*Please tick as applicable below, to confirm the capacity in which the answers are given.* ☐ Managing Agent ☐ Management Company ☐ Landlord ☐ Residents' Association

Note

Additional enquiries. Raise only those specific additional enquiries required to clarify issues arising out of the documents submitted or which are relevant to the management of the Property or which the buyer has expressly requested. Resist raising any general additional enquiries that can be established by the buyer's own enquiries, survey or personal inspection.

Disclaimer

Whilst care has been taken in the preparation of this form, no legal liability is accepted by the organisation which created the form. This disclaimer does not affect the legal responsibilities of the person, or organisation completing this form to answer to the best of their knowledge and ability. If you have any queries you should discuss these with your conveyancer or solicitor.

Second Edition 2015

Fittings and Contents Form (2nd edition)

Address of the property

Postcode ☐☐☐☐☐☐☐

Full names of the seller

Seller's solicitor

Name of solicitors firm

Address

Email

Reference number

Definitions

- 'Seller' means all sellers together where the property is owned by more than one person

- 'Buyer' means all buyers together where the property is being bought by more than one person

The Law Society

www.lawsociety.org.uk

Laserform International 12/10

Instructions to the seller and the buyer

This form must be completed accurately by the seller. It may become part of the contract between the seller and the buyer.

The seller should make a clear statement of what is included in the sale of the property by marking each box in this form with a ✓ or a **X**, as shown below:

Included in the sale of the property	✓
Not included in the sale of the property	**X**

The seller may be prepared to sell to the buyer an item which is otherwise not included in the sale of the property. In this case, the seller should mark the appropriate box with a **X** to show the item is not included, followed by the amount that the seller wishes to be paid for the item, as shown below.

Not included, but for sale at an extra cost	**X**{amount

The buyer can then decide whether to accept the seller's offer. The seller and buyer should inform their solicitors of any arrangements made about items offered for sale in this way.

If the seller removes any fixtures and fittings, the seller must make good any damage caused by their removal.

If the seller removes a light fitting, it is assumed that the seller will replace the fitting with a ceiling rose and socket, a flex, bulb holder and bulb.

The seller is responsible for removing any possessions, including rubbish, from the property, the garage, the garden and any outbuildings or sheds.

The seller and the buyer should check the information given on the form carefully.

1 Basic fittings

Boiler / immersion heater		Roof insulation	
Radiators / wall heaters		Window fitments	
Night-storage heaters		Window shutters / grills	
Free-standing heaters		Internal door furniture	
Gas fires (with surround)		External door furniture	
Electric fires (with surround)		Doorbell / chime	
Light switches		Electric sockets	

2 Television and telephone

Telephone receivers		Television aerial	
Radio aerial		Satellite dish	

3 Kitchen

Hob		Refrigerator / fridge-freezer	
Extractor hood		Freezer	
Fitted oven and grills		Free-standing oven / cooker	
Fitted microwave		Dishwasher	
Tumble-dryer		Washing machine	

4 Bathroom

Bath		Separate shower and fittings	
Shower fitting for bath		Towel rail	
Shower curtain		Soap / toothbrush holders	
Bathroom cabinet		Toilet roll holders	
Taps		Bathroom mirror	

	Carpets	Curtain rails poles/pelmets*	Curtains/ blinds*	Light fittings	Fitted uni*
Hall, stairs and landing					
Living room					
Dining room					
Kitchen					
Bedroom 1					
Bedroom 2					
Bedroom 3					

If the seller wishes to further explain the answers to section 5 above, please give details:

* Delete as appropriate.
** Fitted units (for example: fitted cupboards, fitted shelves, and fitted wardrobes).

Garden furniture		Outdoor heater	
Garden ornaments		Stock of fuel	
Trees, plants, shrubs		Outside lights	
Barbecue		Water butt	
Dustbins		Clothes line	
Garden shed		Rotary line	
Greenhouse			

Signed: .... Dated: ....

Each seller should sign this form.

The Law Society

Law Society Property Information Form (3rd edition)

Address of the property

Postcode ☐☐☐☐☐☐☐

Full names of the seller

Seller's solicitor

Name of solicitor's firm

Address

Email

Reference number

About this form

This form is completed by the seller to supply the detailed information and documents which may be relied upon for the conveyancing process.

It is important that sellers and buyers read the notes below.

Definitions

- 'Seller' means all sellers together where the property is owned by more than one person.
- 'Buyer' means all buyers together where the property is being bought by more than one person.
- 'Property' includes all buildings and land within its boundaries.

The Law Society

www.lawsociety.org.uk

© Law Society 2013
Laserform International 5/13

Instructions to the seller

- The answers should be prepared by the person or persons who are named as owner on the deeds or Land Registry title or by the owner's legal representative(s) if selling under a power of attorney or grant of probate or representation. If there is more than one seller, you should prepare the answers together or, if only one seller prepares the form, the other(s) should check the answers given and all sellers should sign the form.

- If you do not know the answer to any question, you must say so. If you are unsure of the meaning of any questions or answers, please ask your solicitor. Completing this form is not mandatory, but omissions or delay in providing some information may delay the sale.

- If you later become aware of any information which would alter any replies you have given, you must inform your solicitor immediately. This is as important as giving the right answers in the first place. Do not change any arrangements concerning the property with anyone (such as a tenant or neighbour) without first consulting your solicitor.

- It is very important that your answers are accurate. If you give incorrect or incomplete information to the buyer (on this form or otherwise in writing or in conversation, whether through your estate agent or solicitor or directly to the buyer), the buyer may make a claim for compensation from you or refuse to complete the purchase.

- You should answer the questions based upon information known to you (or, in the case of legal representatives, you or the owner). You are not expected to have expert knowledge of legal or technical matters, or matters that occurred prior to your ownership of the property.

- Please give your solicitor any letters, agreements or other papers which help answer the questions. If you are aware of any which you are not supplying with the answers, tell your solicitor. If you do not have any documentation you may need to obtain copies at your own expense. Also pass to your solicitor any notices you have received concerning the property and any which arrive at any time before completion of the sale.

Instructions to the buyer

- If the seller gives you, separately from this form, any information concerning the property (in writing or in conversation, whether through an estate agent or solicitor or directly to you) on which you wish to rely when buying the property, you should tell your solicitor.

- You are entitled to rely on the replies given to enquiries but in relation to the physical condition of the property, the replies should not be treated as a substitute for undertaking your own survey or making your own independent enquiries, which you are recommended to do.

- The seller is only obliged to give answers based on their own information. They may not have knowledge of legal or technical matters. You should not expect the seller to have knowledge of, or give information about, matters prior to their ownership of the property.

If the property is leasehold this section, or parts of it, may not apply.

1.1 Looking towards the property from the road, who owns or accepts responsibility to maintain or repair the boundary features:

(a) on the left?

☐ Seller   ☐ Neighbour
☐ Shared   ☐ Not known

(b) on the right?

☐ Seller   ☐ Neighbour
☐ Shared   ☐ Not known

(c) at the rear?

☐ Seller   ☐ Neighbour
☐ Shared   ☐ Not known

(d) at the front?

☐ Seller   ☐ Neighbour
☐ Shared   ☐ Not known

1.2 If the boundaries are irregular please indicate ownership by written description or by reference to a plan:

1.3 Is the seller aware of any boundary feature having been moved in the last 20 years? If Yes, please give details:

☐ Yes   ☐ No

1.4 During the seller's ownership, has any land previously forming part of the property been sold or has any adjacent property been purchased? If Yes, please give details:

☐ Yes   ☐ No

1.5 Does any part of the property or any building on the property overhang, or project under, the boundary of the neighbouring property or road? If Yes, please give details:

☐ Yes   ☐ No

1.6 Has any notice been received under the Party Wall Act 1996 in respect of any shared/party boundaries? If Yes, please supply a copy, and give details of any works carried out or agreed:

☐ Yes   ☐ No
☐ Enclosed   ☐ To follo

2 **Disputes and complaints**

2.1 Have there been any disputes or complaints regarding this property or a property nearby? If Yes, please give details:

☐ Yes   ☐ No

2.2 Is the seller aware of anything which might lead to a dispute about the property or a property nearby? If Yes, please give details:

☐ Yes   ☐ No

3 **Notices and proposals**

3.1 Have any notices or correspondence been received or sent (e.g. from or to a neighbour, council or government department), or any negotiations or discussions taken place, which affect the property or a property nearby? If Yes, please give details:

☐ Yes   ☐ No

3.2 Is the seller aware of any proposals to develop property or land nearby, or of any proposals to make alterations to buildings nearby? If Yes, please give details:

☐ Yes   ☐ No

Note to seller: All relevant approvals and supporting paperwork referred to in section 4 of this form, such as listed building consents, planning permissions, Building Regulations consents and completion certificates should be provided. If the seller has had works carried out the seller should produce the documentation authorising this. Copies may be obtained from the relevant local authority website. Competent Persons Certificates may be obtained from the contractor or the scheme provider (e.g. FENSA or Gas Safe Register). Further information about Competent Persons Certificates can be found at: **www.gov.uk**.

Note to buyer: If any alterations or improvements have been made since the property was last valued for council tax, the sale of the property may trigger a revaluation. This may mean that following completion of the sale, the property will be put into a higher council tax band. Further information about council tax valuation can be found at: **www.voa.gov.uk**.

4.1 Have any of the following changes been made to the whole or any part of the property (including the garden)?

(a) Building works (e.g. extension, loft or garage conversion, removal of internal walls). If Yes, please give details including dates of all work undertaken:

☐ Yes   ☐ No

(b) Change of use (e.g. from an office to a residence)

☐ Yes   ☐ No
☐ Year

(c) Installation of replacement windows, roof windows, roof lights, glazed doors since 1 April 2002

☐ Yes   ☐ No
☐ Year(s)

(d) Addition of a conservatory

☐ Yes   ☐ No
☐ Year

4.2 If Yes to any of the questions in 4.1 and if the work was undertaken during the seller's ownership of the property:

(a) please supply copies of the planning permissions, Building Regulations approvals and Completion Certificates, OR:

(b) if none were required, please explain why these were not required – e.g. permitted development rights applied or the work was exempt from Building Regulations:

Further information about permitted development can be found at: **www.planningportal.gov.uk**.

4.3 Are any of the works disclosed in 4.1 above unfinished?
If Yes, please give details:

☐ Yes   ☐ No

4.4 Is the seller aware of any breaches of planning permission
conditions or Building Regulations consent conditions,
unfinished work or work that does not have all
necessary consents? If Yes, please give details:

☐ Yes   ☐ No

4.5 Are there any planning or building control issues to resolve?
If Yes, please give details:

☐ Yes   ☐ No

4.6 Have solar panels been installed?

☐ Yes   ☐ No

If Yes:

(a) In what year were the solar panels installed?   [   ] Year

(b) Are the solar panels owned outright?   ☐ Yes   ☐ No

(c) Has a long lease of the roof/air space been granted   ☐ Yes   ☐ No
to a solar panel provider? If Yes, please supply copies   ☐ Enclosed   ☐ To follow
of the relevant documents.

4.7 Is the property or any part of it:

(a) a listed building?   ☐ Yes   ☐ No
☐ Not known

(b) in a conservation area?   ☐ Yes   ☐ No
☐ Not known

If Yes, please supply copies of any relevant documents.   ☐ Enclosed   ☐ To follow

4.8 Are any of the trees on the property subject to a
Tree Preservation Order?

☐ Yes   ☐ No
☐ Not known

If Yes:

(a) Have the terms of the Order been complied with?

☐ Yes   ☐ No
☐ Not known

(b) Please supply a copy of any relevant documents.

☐ Enclosed   ☐ To follow

5 Guarantees and warranties

Note to seller: All available guarantees, warranties and supporting paperwork should be supplied
before exchange of contracts.

Note to buyer: Some guarantees only operate to protect the person who had the work carried out or
may not be valid if their terms have been breached. You may wish to contact the company to establish
whether it is still trading and if so, whether the terms of the guarantee will apply to you.

5.1 Does the property benefit from any of the following guarantees or warranties? If Yes, please
supply a copy.

(a) New home warranty (e.g. NHBC or similar)

☐ Yes   ☐ No
☐ Enclosed   ☐ To follow

(b) Damp proofing

☐ Yes   ☐ No
☐ Enclosed   ☐ To follow

(c) Timber treatment

☐ Yes   ☐ No
☐ Enclosed   ☐ To follow

(d) Windows, roof lights, roof windows or glazed doors

☐ Yes   ☐ No
☐ Enclosed   ☐ To follow

(e) Electrical work

☐ Yes   ☐ No
☐ Enclosed   ☐ To follow

(f) Roofing

☐ Yes   ☐ No
☐ Enclosed   ☐ To follow

(g)   Central heating

☐ Yes   ☐ No
☐ Enclosed   ☐ To follow

(h)   Underpinning

☐ Yes   ☐ No
☐ Enclosed   ☐ To follow

(i)   Other (please state):

☐ Enclosed   ☐ To follow

5.2 Have any claims been made under any of these guarantees or warranties? If Yes, please give details:

☐ Yes   ☐ No

6.1 Does the seller insure the property?

☐ Yes   ☐ No

6.2 Has any buildings insurance taken out by the seller ever been:

(a)   subject to an abnormal rise in premiums?

☐ Yes   ☐ No

(b)   subject to high excesses?

☐ Yes   ☐ No

(c)   subject to unusual conditions?

☐ Yes   ☐ No

(d)   refused?

☐ Yes   ☐ No

If Yes, please give details:

6.3 Has the seller made any buildings insurance claims? If Yes, please give details:

☐ Yes   ☐ No

Flooding

Note: Flooding may take a variety of forms: it may be seasonal or irregular or simply a one-off occurrence. The property does not need to be near a sea or river for flooding to occur. Further information about flooding can be found at: **www.defra.gov.uk**.

7.1 Has any part of the property (whether buildings or surrounding garden or land) ever been flooded? If Yes, please state when the flooding occurred and identify the parts that flooded:

☐ Yes ☐ No

If No to question 7.1 please continue to 7.3 and do not answer 7.2 below.

7.2 What type of flooding occurred?

(a)	Ground water	☐ Yes	☐ No
(b)	Sewer flooding	☐ Yes	☐ No
(c)	Surface water	☐ Yes	☐ No
(d)	Coastal flooding	☐ Yes	☐ No
(e)	River flooding	☐ Yes	☐ No

(f)　Other (please state):

7.3 Has a Flood Risk Report been prepared? If Yes, please supply a copy.

☐ Yes　☐ No
☐ Enclosed　☐ To follow

Further information about the types of flooding and Flood Risk Reports can be found at: **www.environment-agency.gov.uk**.

Radon

Note: Radon is a naturally occurring inert radioactive gas found in the ground. Some parts of England and Wales are more adversely affected by it than others. Remedial action is advised for properties with a test result above the 'recommended action level'. Further information about Radon can be found at: **www.hpa.org.uk**.

7.4 Has a Radon test been carried out on the property?

☐ Yes　☐ No

If Yes:

(a)	please supply a copy of the report	☐ Enclosed	☐ To follow
(b)	was the test result below the 'recommended action level'?	☐ Yes	☐ No

7.5 Were any remedial measures undertaken on construction to reduce Radon gas levels in the property?

☐ Yes ☐ No
☐ Not known

Energy efficiency

Note: An Energy Performance Certificate (EPC) is a document that gives information about a property's energy usage. Further information about EPCs can be found at: **www.gov.uk**.

7.6 Please supply a copy of the EPC for the property.

☐ Enclosed ☐ To follow
☐ Already supplied

7.7 Have any installations in the property been financed under the Green Deal scheme? If Yes, please give details of all installations and supply a copy of your last electricity bill.

☐ Yes ☐ No
☐ Enclosed ☐ To follow

Further information about the Green Deal can be found at: **www.gov.uk/decc**.

Japanese knotweed

Note: Japanese knotweed is an invasive plant that can cause damage to property. It can take several years to eradicate.

7.8 Is the property affected by Japanese knotweed?

☐ Yes ☐ No
☐ Not known

If Yes, please state whether there is a Japanese knotweed management plan in place and supply a copy.

☐ Yes ☐ No
☐ Not known
☐ Enclosed ☐ To follow

Note: Rights and arrangements may relate to access or shared use. They may also include leases of less than seven years, rights to mines and minerals, manorial rights, chancel repair and similar matters. If you are uncertain about whether a right or arrangement is covered by this question, please ask your solicitor.

8.1 Does ownership of the property carry a responsibility to contribute towards the cost of any jointly used services, such as maintenance of a private road, a shared driveway, a boundary or drain? If Yes, please give details:

☐ Yes ☐ No

8.2 Does the property benefit from any rights or arrangements over any neighbouring property? If Yes, please give details:

☐ Yes   ☐ No

8.3 Has anyone taken steps to prevent access to the property, or to complain about or demand payment for access to the property? If Yes, please give details:

☐ Yes   ☐ No

8.4 Does the seller know of any of the following rights or arrangements which affect the property?

(a) Rights of light	☐ Yes	☐ No
(b) Rights of support from adjoining properties	☐ Yes	☐ No
(c) Customary rights (e.g. rights deriving from local traditions)	☐ Yes	☐ No
(d) Other people's rights to mines and minerals under the land	☐ Yes	☐ No
(e) Chancel repair liability	☐ Yes	☐ No
(f) Other people's rights to take things from the land (such as timber, hay or fish)	☐ Yes	☐ No

If Yes, please give details:

8.5 Are there any other rights or arrangements affecting the property? If Yes, please give details:

☐ Yes   ☐ No

Services crossing the property or neighbouring property

8.6 Do any drains, pipes or wires serving the property cross any neighbour's property?

☐ Yes   ☐ No
☐ Not known

8.7 Do any drains, pipes or wires leading to any neighbour's property cross the property?

☐ Yes   ☐ No
☐ Not known

8.8 Is there any agreement or arrangement about drains, pipes or wires?

☐ Yes   ☐ No
☐ Not known

If Yes, please supply a copy or give details:

☐ Enclosed   ☐ To follow

---

9 Parking

9.1 What are the parking arrangements at the property?

9.2 Is the property in a controlled parking zone or within a local authority parking scheme?

☐ Yes   ☐ No
☐ Not known

---

10 Other charges

Note: If the property is leasehold, details of lease expenses such as service charges and ground re should be set out on the separate TA7 Leasehold Information Form. If the property is freehold, ther may still be charges: for example, payments to a management company or for the use of a private drainage system.

10.1 Does the seller have to pay any charges relating to the property (excluding any payments such as council tax, utility charges, etc.), for example payments to a management company? If Yes, please give details:

☐ Yes   ☐ No

---

11 Occupiers

11.1 Does the seller live at the property?

☐ Yes   ☐ No

11.2 Does anyone else, aged 17 or over, live at the property?

☐ Yes   ☐ No

If No to question 11.2, please continue to section 12 'Services' and do not answer 11.3–11.5 below.

11.3 Please give the full names of any occupiers (other than the sellers) aged 17 or over:

11.4 Are any of the occupiers (other than the sellers), aged 17 or over, tenants or lodgers? ☐ Yes ☐ No

11.5 Is the property being sold with vacant possession? ☐ Yes ☐ No

If Yes, have all the occupiers aged 17 or over:

(a) agreed to leave prior to completion? ☐ Yes ☐ No

(b) agreed to sign the sale contract? If No, please supply other evidence that the property will be vacant on completion. ☐ Yes ☐ No ☐ Enclosed ☐ To follow

12 Services

Note: If the seller does not have a certificate requested below this can be obtained from the relevant Competent Persons Scheme. Further information about Competent Persons Schemes can be found at: **www.gov.uk**.

Electricity

12.1 Has the whole or any part of the electrical installation been tested by a qualified and registered electrician? ☐ Yes ☐ No

If Yes, please state the year it was tested and provide a copy of the test certificate. ☐ ____ Year ☐ Enclosed ☐ To follow

12.2 Has the property been rewired or had any electrical installation work carried out since 1 January 2005? ☐ Yes ☐ No ☐ Not known

If Yes, please supply one of the following:

(a) a copy of the signed BS7671 Electrical Safety Certificate ☐ Enclosed ☐ To follow

(b) the installer's Building Regulations Compliance Certificate ☐ Enclosed ☐ To follow

(c) the Building Control Completion Certificate ☐ Enclosed ☐ To follow

Central heating

12.3 Does the property have a central heating system? ☐ Yes ☐ No

If Yes:

(a) What type of system is it (e.g. mains gas, liquid gas, oil, electricity, etc.)?

[_____]

(b) When was the heating system installed? If on or after 1 April 2005 please supply a copy of the 'completion certificate' (e.g. CORGI or Gas Safe Register) or the 'exceptional circumstances' form.

[_____] D

☐ Not known

☐ Enclosed ☐ To follow

(c) Is the heating system in good working order? ☐ Yes ☐ No

(d) In what year was the heating system last serviced/maintained? Please supply a copy of the inspection report.

[_____] Year ☐ Not know

☐ Enclosed ☐ To follow

☐ Not available

Drainage and sewerage

Note: Further information about drainage and sewerage can be found at: **www.environment-agency.gov.uk**.

12.4 Is the property connected to mains:

(a) foul water drainage? ☐ Yes ☐ No

☐ Not known

(b) surface water drainage? ☐ Yes ☐ No

☐ Not known

If Yes to both questions in 12.4, please continue to section 13 'Connection to utilities and services' and do not answer 12.5–12.10 below.

12.5 Is sewerage for the property provided by:

(a) a septic tank? ☐ Yes ☐ No

(b) a sewage treatment plant? ☐ Yes ☐ No

(c) cesspool? ☐ Yes ☐ No

12.6 Is the use of the septic tank, sewage treatment plant or cesspool shared with other properties? If Yes, how many properties share the system?

☐ Yes ☐ No

[_____] Properties share

12.7 When was the system last emptied?

[   ] Year

12.8 If the property is served by a sewage treatment plant, when was the treatment plant last serviced?

[   ] Year

12.9 When was the system installed?

[   ] Year

Note: Some systems installed after 1 January 1991 require Building Regulations approval, environmental permits or registration. Further information about permits and registration can be found at: **www.environment-agency.gov.uk**.

12.10 Is any part of the septic tank, sewage treatment plant (including any soakaway or outfall) or cesspool, or the access to it, outside the boundary of the property? If Yes, please supply a plan showing the location of the system and how access is obtained.

☐ Yes   ☐ No
☐ Enclosed   ☐ To follow

13 Connection to utilities and services

Please mark the Yes or No boxes to show which of the following utilities and services are connected to the property and give details of any providers.

Mains electricity   Yes ☐ No ☐

Provider's name

[   ]

Location of meter

[   ]

Mains gas   Yes ☐ No ☐

Provider's name

[   ]

Location of meter

[   ]

Mains water   Yes ☐ No ☐

Provider's name

[   ]

Location of stopcock

[   ]

Location of meter, if any

[   ]

Mains sewerage   Yes ☐ No ☐

Provider's name

[   ]

Telephone   Yes ☐ No ☐

Provider's name

[   ]

Cable   Yes ☐ No ☐

Provider's name

[   ]

14.1 Is this sale dependent on the seller completing the purchase of another property on the same day? ☐ Yes ☐ No

14.2 Does the seller have any special requirements about a moving date? If Yes, please give details: ☐ Yes ☐ No

14.3 Does the sale price exceed the amount necessary to repay all mortgages and charges secured on the property? ☐ Yes ☐ No

14.4 Will the seller ensure that:

(a) all rubbish is removed from the property (including from the loft, garden, outbuildings, garages and sheds) and that the property will be left in a clean and tidy condition? ☐ Yes ☐ No

(b) if light fittings are removed, the fittings will be replaced with ceiling rose, flex, bulb holder and bulb? ☐ Yes ☐ No

(c) reasonable care will be taken when removing any other fittings or contents? ☐ Yes ☐ No

(d) keys to all windows and doors and details of alarm codes will be left at the property or with the estate agent? ☐ Yes ☐ No

Signed: .... Dated: ....

Signed: .... Dated: ....

Each seller should sign this form.

The Law Society is the representative body for solicitors in England and Wales.

Leasehold information form

Document date ☐☐ / ☐☐ / ☐☐

Address of the property

Postcode ☐☐☐☐☐☐☐☐

This form should be completed and read in conjunction with the explanatory notes available separately

1 Other leases

1.1 Is there any headlease?

If Yes, please supply a copy.

☐ Yes ☐ No ☐ Enclosed
☐ To follow ☐ Not known

1.2 Is there any underlease?

If Yes, please supply a copy.

☐ Yes ☐ No ☐ Enclosed
☐ To follow ☐ Not known

1.3 In respect of any headlease or underlease of the whole or any part of the property, state any amounts owing or owed by or to the seller relating to rent, service charge, insurance premiums or other financial contribution.

The Law Society

www.hips.lawsociety.org.uk

TA7
© Law Society 2007
Laserform International 8/07

2 Management company

2.1 Is there a management company which is run by the tenants?

☐ Yes   ☐ No

If Yes, please supply copies of the following:

(a) Memorandum and articles of association

☐ Enclosed   ☐ To follow

(b) The share or membership certificate

☐ Enclosed   ☐ To follow

(c) The company's accounts for the last three years

☐ Enclosed   ☐ To follow

(d) The names and addresses of the secretary and treasurer of the company:

2.2 Has the management company been dissolved or removed from the register at Companies House?

☐ Yes   ☐ No

3 Maintenance charges

3.1 Have there been any problems in the last three years between flat owners and the landlord or management company about maintenance charges, or the method of management?

☐ Yes   ☐ No

If Yes, please give details:

3.2 Has there been any challenge to the maintenance charges or any expense in the last three years?

☐ Yes   ☐ No

If Yes, please give details:

3.3 Has the landlord had any problems with collecting the maintenance charges from other flat owners?

☐ Yes ☐ No

If Yes, please give details:

4.1 Has a notice been received from any landlord or landlord's agent?

☐ Yes ☐ No ☐ Enclosed ☐ To follow

If Yes, please supply a copy.

4.2 Has any other notice been received from any other person or authority?

☐ Yes ☐ No ☐ Enclosed ☐ To follow

If Yes, please supply a copy.

4.3 Are any changes to the terms of the lease proposed or has the landlord given any consents under the lease? (This could be in a formal document, a letter or even oral).

☐ Yes ☐ No ☐ Enclosed ☐ To follow

If Yes, please give details or supply a copy.

4.4 Please provide the name and address of the landlord or landlord's agent for service of any notice of change of ownership.

☐ To follow ☐ Not applicable

Note: A notice could be on a printed form or in the form of a letter and a buyer will wish to know if anything of this sort has been received.

5 Complaints

5.1 Has the seller received any complaint from the landlord, any other landlord, management company or any other occupier about anything the seller has or has not done? ☐ Yes ☐ No

If Yes, please give details:

> (blank box)

5.2 Has the seller complained or does the seller have cause for complaint to or about the landlord, management company or any other occupier? ☐ Yes ☐ No

If Yes, please give details:

> (blank box)

6 Buildings insurance of the property

6.1 Is the seller responsible under the terms of the lease for arranging the buildings insurance of the property? ☐ Yes ☐ No

If Yes, please supply copies of:

(a) the insurance policy ☐ Enclosed ☐ To follow

(b) the receipt for the last payment of the premium ☐ Enclosed ☐ To follow

6.2 Is the landlord or management company responsible for arranging the buildings insurance of the property? ☐ Yes ☐ No

If Yes, please supply copies of:

(a) the insurance policy ☐ Enclosed ☐ To follow

(b) the schedule for the current year ☐ Enclosed ☐ To follow

6.3 Do the insurers record the interests of the buyer's mortgagee and the buyer on the policy? ☐ Yes ☐ No ☐ Not known

7 Decoration

7.1 When was the outside of the building last decorated? In the year [ ] ☐ Not known

7.2 When were any internal communal parts last decorated? In the year [ ] ☐ Not known

7.3 When was the inside of the property last decorated? In the year [ ] ☐ Not known

8 Alterations

8.1 Is the seller aware of any alterations having been made to the property since the lease was originally granted? ☐ Yes ☐ No ☐ Not known

If Yes, please give details:

[ ]

8.2 If alterations have been made to the property since the lease was originally granted, was the landlord's consent obtained?

If Yes, please supply copies of any consents obtained.

☐ Yes ☐ No
☐ Enclosed ☐ To follow
☐ Not known ☐ Not required

9 Occupation

9.1 Is the seller now occupying the property as their sole or main home? ☐ Yes ☐ No

9.2 Has the seller occupied the property as their sole or main home (apart from usual holidays and business trips):

(a) continuously throughout the last 12 months? ☐ Yes ☐ No

(b) continuously throughout the last three years? ☐ Yes ☐ No

(c) for periods totalling at least three years during the last 10 years? ☐ Yes ☐ No

Leasehold information form TA7

10.1 Has the seller served on the landlord or any other person a notice under the enfranchisement legislation stating the desire to buy the freehold or be granted an extended lease?

☐ Yes   ☐ No   ☐ Enclosed
☐ To follow

If Yes, please supply a copy.

10.2 If the property is a flat in a block, is the seller aware of the service of any notice under the enfranchisement legislation relating to the possible collective purchase of the freehold of the block or part of it?

☐ Yes   ☐ No   ☐ Enclosed
☐ To follow

If Yes, please supply a copy.

10.3 Has the seller received any response to that notice?

☐ Yes   ☐ No   ☐ Enclosed
☐ To follow

If Yes, please supply a copy.

The information in this form has been given by:

Name

The Law Society

This form is part of the Law Society's TransAction scheme.
The Law Society is the representative body for solicitors in England and Wales.
Laserform International Ltd is an Approved Law Society Supplier